blue
rider
press

I AM DURÁN

I AM DURÁN

MY AUTOBIOGRAPHY

ROBERTO DURÁN

with George Diaz

BLUE RIDER PRESS

New York

blue
rider
press

An imprint of Penguin Random House LLC
375 Hudson Street
New York, New York 10014

ISBN 9780735213128

Printed in the United States of America
1   3   5   7   9   10   8   6   4   2

Book design by Marysarah Quinn

I want to dedicate this book to all of my family and the people of Panama. They are my everything.

CONTENTS

PROLOGUE

I DIED ON AN OPERATING TABLE in a hospital in Buenos Aires. I was dead for thirty seconds. That's what I'm told, anyway.

On October 4, 2001, I was in a bad car crash with my son Chavo. We'd left Panama the day before to attend a music promotion in Argentina that he was involved in. I wanted to help him out, even though I wasn't keen on going. I'd already arranged to go to Vancouver to see my friend José Sulaimán, the president of the World Boxing Council, and I was going to take one of my daughters, Irichelle; I'd never really spent much time with her over the last few years. But Chavo was persistent. "Please, Papi!" he kept saying.

"I don't want to go," I remember telling him. "I've got a bad feeling about it."

The flight there was a little bumpy. I shook my head— "*Qué te dije?*" I said to him. What did I tell you?

In Buenos Aires we went straight to a nice restaurant and

spent the evening doing the things I love most—eating, drinking, having a great time. Chavo was watching a soccer game on TV there, and he suddenly got the urge to see the second half in person. He asked where the game was being played. Not far at all, he was told.

"Let's go!" he said.

"Screw it," I told him. "I want to stay here with my wine and my champagne and my churrasco."

"Vamos, vamos, vamos!"

The reason Chavo was so excited was that some soccer star named Ariel Ortega was playing—a midfielder, whose nickname was "El Burrito." I didn't know much about him, but I did know I wanted to stay where I was, drinking champagne.

"Please, Papi, please! It's not the same if you don't come! I want you to meet El Burrito!"

"I got your Burrito right here," I said, grabbing my crotch. "Go on your own."

"It'd be much better with you," said Chavo. "We'll get in more quickly."

So off we went. By now, it wasn't just dark, it was raining hard, too. I can't remember much of what happened, but before we got to the stadium we got hit by a car from behind and both cars crashed into a wall. *Bang!* Had our driver let up on the gas pedal, I think we would have been okay, but he kept his foot down and the car went spinning along those wide streets they have in Buenos Aires. If we hadn't hit that barrier, we'd have crashed into a bunch of other cars and died right there.

I braced my hand against the front seat and saw I was bleeding badly. I felt groggy. My other hand, it looked broken. But the worst part was that the guy sitting next to me had gone flying across the seat and hit me very hard. I ended up with a collapsed lung and eight broken ribs. I was bleeding from my mouth, too, which made it hard to breathe. At least all the wine and champagne I'd had to drink meant it didn't hurt so much.

They put me in a neck brace and rushed me to the hospital. I was in a daze when we got there—one of the doctors in the corridor was screaming, "I have Durán's watch! I have the watch of Manos de Piedra!"

I was mostly worried about my son. "Where's Chavo?" I kept screaming. "Where's Chavo?" Please, I prayed to God, it's okay to take me, but not him—please, not him. Then I saw him, with an IV line dangling from his arm. He was hurt, too, but not as bad as me, although he pissed blood for three days.

In Panama, however, they killed me off. News got around that I'd had an accident, and before I could say anything they were reporting that I'd been killed in the crash. The rumors sent the country into a frenzy. They thought I was gone, and they started selling sweaters, key chains, trinkets, souvenirs—all sorts of crap with my name or photo on it. Back in the hospital I laughed my ass off.

It wasn't so funny for my family back home, though. The day after the accident, my brother Pototo opened the door to a neighbor who said, "Are you watching the news about your brother? He's in critical condition"—and from that moment they'd been desperate for news. Pototo didn't know what to do, so he called my wife, Fula. At least Fula was able to fly to Buenos Aires and calm everyone down.

It turned out one of the ribs had punctured my lung, which led to water on the lung, so the doctors kept me in the hospital to operate on me once the bruising and swelling had gone down. And then I got an infection.

That, I was told later, was when I went into cardiac arrest for two or three minutes. If it had been anyone else, the doctor said, I would have stayed dead. But my good health and physical strength meant I didn't die, thank God.

When I came around, everything was white. *Chuleta!* I thought I *had* died. "Am I in heaven?" I cried.

"Not yet, Cholo," said an old guy next to me. "Not yet!"

Then the doctor gave it to me straight: my lung had suffered a lot of damage and I should consider myself lucky to be alive. "Durán, no more fighting. You've got to retire." I wasn't going to argue with the doctors.

I was finally able to go home on November 16, nearly six weeks after the accident, and the doctors told me I needed another four months to fully recuperate. It had been really, really rough—I'd cried because of the pain.

And so, in January 2002, I retired. I guess I was okay with leaving the sport like that, though before the accident I'd never given any thought to retiring, not even a few months earlier when I'd lost to Héctor "Macho" Camacho. If I hadn't been hurt so badly in that accident, I don't know if I would have continued fighting. In fact, being in good shape from that Camacho fight is probably what saved me in the crash.

But even though I was fifty when I retired, I would gladly have beaten the crap out of all the deadbeats in the sport. The same goes with the boxers today: Pacquiao, Mayweather—they're pitiful. I could have beaten all of them.

Throughout my entire boxing career—thirty-three years—I never thought anyone could beat me. I never thought bad things would happen to me in the ring. I was going to win or I was going to knock someone out—I did a lot of that. Just look at my record. I beat the American idol, Sugar Ray Leonard. Knocked out Puerto Rico's hero, Esteban de Jesús. Wilfred Benítez. Iran Barkley—people thought Barkley was going to kill me. I nearly killed him. Remembering things like that makes me laugh.

My strategy was very simple. In my personal life I am not an animal, but in the ring there was an animal inside me. Sometimes it roared the moment the first bell rang. Sometimes it sprang out later in the fight. But I could always feel it there, driving me and pushing me forward. It's what made me win, what made me enjoy fighting.

The worst thing you could do with me was be scared, because I'd smell that fear. I never feared anyone, even when I was a kid. I grew up on the streets, and after the childhood I had, who the fuck was I going to be scared of? I fought in the streets before I ever fought in the gym. I'd go to the corner and tell Plomo, my first trainer, "He hit me hard, but I'm going to hit him harder." Plomo saw that instinct. The streets taught me everything I needed to know about life and boxing.

Boxing has given me everything. I've met the rich and famous. Frank Sinatra, Bob Hope, Sylvester Stallone, Robert De Niro, Diego Maradona. I've traveled the world. New York, Las Vegas, Atlantic City, Montreal, London, China. Panamanians love me. They *adore* me. I'm an idol in my country, but sometimes I think the gringos love me even more. I've been honored by presidents—great presidents like Nelson Mandela. Partied in limousines and private planes chartered by the government. I've slept in Panama's presidential palace. Dined and gotten drunk with Hollywood stars, played and sung with some of the Latin salsa greats. I've bought dozens of cars, drunk the best wines, eaten delicious steaks. Boxing gave me all that, and more. So I drink a lot sometimes—so what? Life's meant to be enjoyed, and mine's been a party. *La jodienda*, Latin people call it.

Boxing is part of my life, but so are my family and friends. It's tough to keep it all in focus all the time from when you're a *pelao*, a kid, to when you're a man touching fifty who's still fighting for his family, for his pride, for all those fans—for the joy of being respected by the people he cares about.

I'm a family man who loves his wife, but I've also slept around and fathered other children. I make no apologies for that. As world champion, as one of the most famous and honored men in Panama, I've been around temptation every day, and I'm not going to say sorry for the things I've done. Thank God I have a beautiful, intelligent, forgiving, loving wife. I also have five beautiful children with Fula—three boys and two girls. They're everything to me—gifts of God.

You'll always find me in a good mood. And if I do get in a bad mood, I'll snap out of it in an instant. Maybe that's why I've always struggled to make weight. When you're a world champion and have achieved all you want, it's hard to keep engaged. I'd fight, then drink, party, and gain weight. I'd have to lose twenty, thirty pounds in a month—it was like shedding tears of blood. And I'd still win. I loved to box, but I also loved the other things in life and I was never going to deny myself. It drove my trainers and managers crazy. But they weren't the ones out there busting their asses in the gym and winning all those fights. I was the one who made them famous, not the other way around.

Just look at my record. Over a hundred victories, seventy by knockout. Five world titles in four different divisions. I was a world champion at twenty-one. A champion again at thirty-seven. I fought into five decades, from 1968 to 2001. People rate me as the greatest lightweight of all time. And why not? I think I am. "There is only one legend," as I've often said, "and that's me."

Manos de Piedra. Hands of Stone. El Cholo.

ONE

STREET

FIGHTING

MAN

I AM A CHILD OF THE STREETS. My neighbors were thieves, whores, and murderers. My father wasn't around and I never made it past third grade. I still don't read or write much, but I know what poverty is, because my childhood sucked. *Mierda*. Shit.

To this day I believe that boxing champions never come from rich neighborhoods. They come from the barrios, the gutters—it's God's law. God wrote the script for me before I was born. All I had to do was follow the path He set for me. It wasn't an easy one. Sometimes I had to sleep on the streets with a newspaper for a blanket. Good weather, bad weather, didn't matter; rain or hot as hell. "A gypsy," my manager Carlos Eleta once called me. "He likes to be free." Okay, a gypsy, but I survived.

When you're a *pelao*—the nickname they give street kids in Panama—you don't think about what you have or don't have. You live from day to day—every fucking day. You struggle to find food to eat. You struggle to keep your brothers and sisters safe. I was too young to process any of this at the time, of course, and even now I don't think much about it, but I know it's there, and even when I became rich I never forgot where I'd come from. I didn't have any toys, no fancy trucks for my birthday, no fancy clothes. None of that shit. It was all about *lo que necesitas*—what you need.

I was born into the arms of my grandmother, doña Ceferina García, on June 16, 1951, and given the name Roberto Durán Samaniego. My mother was late for everything, and she couldn't even get to the hospital in time. When the contractions started, she stayed home, and so I was born at Casa de Piedra, Avenida A (no. 147), Cuarto 96, in El Chorrillo, a working-class neighborhood down by the water in Panama City, not far from the entrance to the Panama Canal.

Panama in the 1950s was a rough country, not like now. The government didn't give a shit about stuff like education and keeping people safe. The Panama Canal was causing a lot of tension. Students were demonstrating against the United States and getting into fights with the National Guard. There was a lot of violence, rioting—nothing for the people but despair and poverty. When I was born, you arrived in the world naked and had to look after yourself immediately, because no one else was going to do it. Just ask my mother.

My mother, Clara Esther Samaniego, was Panamanian, but my dad, Margarito Durán Sánchez, was a soldier with Mexican and Cherokee blood. He made me and then left when I was one and a half. I wouldn't see him for another twenty years, when I was fighting professionally in Los Angeles, and then I didn't see him again. All those years he was gone from my life I didn't spend a lot of time thinking about him. Why should I have? He was nothing to me.

My dad met my mother when he was working as a cook with the United States Army in the Panama Canal Zone. She was twenty then, and before he left he would father another son, Alcibíades, with her, but this child died of a heart problem when he was two. He was buried in a cemetery for poor families—we barely had enough money for food, so how were we going to afford a tombstone? My mother already had another son, Domingo ("Toti"), from a relationship with a Puerto Rican man, and a daughter, Marina, from a relationship with a Filipino. Life wasn't easy, but she didn't make it any easier for herself or us.

There were definitely no fancy homes in El Chorrillo, just wooden tenements—slums, even—and lots and lots of bars. Most people who lived there were immigrants working on the construction of the Panama Canal, mainly from the Caribbean, which was even poorer than Panama back then. There were some bad people there, guys who hustled for money by stealing cigarettes and beer from the U.S. military bases, but there were some good people, too, teachers and clerks, who looked out for us kids.

I didn't go to school much because I didn't have to. I wasn't interested, so there wasn't much point. When I did go, I'd just have breakfast and then leave, since we didn't have money for anything. I had this little box that contained stuff to shine shoes with, and I'd go home from school, change my clothes, and go out again to shine shoes. And that's how I started my life—shining shoes on the pavement when I should have been at school.

It was just as well I didn't spend much time at school, because whenever I did go I ended up getting into fights and getting kicked out. Back then, I was more of a wrestler, preferring to pin people to the floor, but even then, just like in the ring, I never backed down. It wasn't my fault, though. The kids from the fifth and sixth grades would always pick on the *pelaos* from the first grade. So one day a sixth-grader started picking on a first-grader. I jumped in, decked the sixth-grader, and left him gasping for air. They took me to the principal's office and this time they kicked me out of school for good. My mother took me to another school and the same thing happened. In the end I stopped going to school altogether, and every morning I'd leave the house to shine shoes and sell newspapers with my older brother Toti.

I call it home, but there was nothing there for me. No dad, and a mother who wasn't very interested in me. She'd get tired of looking after me and send me off to Guararé, where my grandmother lived. That was about 150 miles away, so I'd have to get in this fucking truck used to transport chickens. For eight fucking hours. *Chuleta!* And my grandmother was just as bad. Whenever I turned up she tried to palm me off on other relatives, and if they wouldn't have me, then on her friends. She always told me there were too many kids and not enough money. It was true—there were days when we had no food, nothing to eat, and as a result we learned early in life to fend for ourselves. From the moment I started running in the streets I was helping my mother, Toti, my sister, and my other brothers and sisters—together we did what we could just to stay alive.

I would do anything to try to get money for my family, even though I was only a child. I'd go out and chop wood and then use the money to buy milk and rice, and that's what we'd have to eat that day. But my family was only one of many who had this kind of life. There were a lot of *pelaos* just like me. One of the religious groups would raise funds for a Christmas party for the *pelaos* by selling raffle tickets for two dollars. The prize was a gallon of Johnnie Walker Black. A lot of men bought those tickets.

We'd jump the fence into the fancy part of the neighborhood called La Zona to look for food in dumpsters. People who had more money, and the gringos who worked on the Canal, they'd throw away the food they didn't want, which was great for us. Those days when we could all eat properly were real celebrations!

I eventually met a street performer and hustler named Chaflán—that's what everyone called him; his real name was Cándido Natalio Díaz. Everybody said Chaflán was crazy, but he was a good guy and, for me, he was a legend. He wore a sailor's hat around town, dancing at the cantinas. There would always be ten or fifteen kids with Chaflán, including me, following him everywhere. We'd jostle around him, making faces while he danced, doing flips in the air, handstands, hoping people would throw money at our feet. He knew what it took to get the nickels and dimes—that's why we stuck with him.

It was spending so much time with Chaflán that made my arms so strong. Every day I'd be performing—standing on my arms and doing flips, performing tricks and hoping passersby would throw us a dime or two. We were still street urchins—they called me Cholo or Cholito, because of my mixed Indian and white heritage; I had my father's nose as well as his blood. Sometimes when he'd made enough money Chaflán would take us to the beach and buy us lunch. Afterward, he'd make us wrestle until we were covered in sand. Back then, wrestling was very popular, and a lot of wrestlers would come to Panama. We'd wash the sand off in the sea and then go to a Spanish restaurant called El Gato Negro, where we'd have shrimp, yellow rice, and a glass of water, and we were good to go.

We figured out ways to make ten cents here and there hustling in the streets. Chaflán would gather seven or eight kids to sell newspapers on Avenida 4 de Julio, and we'd get up really early and go with him to where *La Estrella de Panamá* would come rolling off the presses around five a.m. There was a window where you picked up the papers, and the first kids to get their bundles would sell them fast, but it was harder for little kids like us. The bigger kids always outmuscled us and got to sell more.

When we weren't selling newspapers, Toti and I would shine shoes in a place called Calle Gota. When the American soldiers working on the Panama Canal left to go party and chase prostitutes, we would hustle them. The first English word I learned was "shoeshine." That's what I used say to all the gringos to hustle a dime or a quarter: "Shoeshine? Shoeshine?"

It worked like this: I shined shoes while Toti kept a lookout, because there was always a guard at the corner of the street, even at midnight. If the police came, he'd shout, "Cops!" and we'd go hide behind a building. Sometimes we'd get caught and have to go to juvenile court, maybe spend the night in jail, before they released us the next day. The cops were always harassing us street kids, putting us in jail for petty offenses, but we didn't care: as soon as they let us out we would go shine shoes again. Same shit, every day. We'd get our ten cents a pair, and every so often when I'd gotten five dimes together I'd go to the movies. The rest I'd always give to my mother, because she had mouths to feed and needed it more than I did.

I'd take the money and go to our local church, the Iglesia de Santa Ana, to light candles for my brothers and sisters and ask the saints to protect them. If I had the money, I would light a candle for each of them, a dime at a time. I would honor all saints—I didn't have a favorite until my mother made me honor hers, the Virgen del Carmen. She is patroness and protector of all seamen and fishermen. Years later, I remember, I was going to a pre-fight press conference in Cleveland with my former manager, Luis de Cubas, when the flight got really, really rocky. "Don't worry," I told him. "When I was small, I shined shoes every day to help out my mother and brothers. But before I went back home, I always went to church to light a candle for my family so God would help them. God is always going to do right by me. We're not going to die." And I was right.

When I was growing up, nothing much changed from one day to another. I hustled for small change. I sold the newspaper. Sometimes I worked in a store, cutting ice and distributing it. Thank God I wasn't a thief, and I've never smoked in my life. Even then I liked a drink now and again, but, though I saw them every day, I never went in for drugs—I am proud of that.

When I wasn't shining shoes or selling newspapers, I'd wake up at five a.m. and wait for the market to open. The elderly people who shopped there were often frail, so Toti and I would hold their bags for them while they did their shopping, and when the bags were good and full, we'd carry them to their cars or back to their homes. Then we'd get tips, five or ten cents. There was a lady who sold *chicha*, a drink made from corn, and *arepas*, a flatbread made from ground maize. Once I'd made my first ten cents, I'd buy an *arepa* and a drink.

My other treat would be movies. I loved the pictures and went whenever I could. I'd watch anything—action movies, Blue Devil cartoons, *King Kong*, cowboy movies, horror movies like *Zombie Versus the Mummy*, and movies featuring my favorite Mexican wrestlers: El Santo, El Vampiro, Huracán Ramírez, and Black Shadow. Even if the movies were in English and I didn't understand a word, I still loved them! The theater would open around one p.m., and it cost twenty-five cents to get in. After the first screening, I'd ask the person in the box office if I could go out and get back in, and then I'd go to a restaurant and beg for bread and water, which I could get for free. I'd go back to the theater with the bread in a bag and watch another movie. There were a couple of places I loved going to: Teatro Presidente and Teatro Tropical. At the Teatro Presidente, I once met Miguel Manzano, a famous Mexican actor. He came out and I said, "Can I clean your shoes?"

"How much?"

"Ten cents."

So he reached into his pocket, pulled out some Panamanian coins, and I pointed to the right one.

At the Teatro Tropical, I met Demetrio González, a film actor and singer of ranchera music, and I met another famous actor at the Teatro Apolo. I paid thirty-five cents to watch the show, and I asked him if I could wear the big Mexican hat he had on.

"Put it on, son," he said. I thought that was very cool. I must have been ten years old—I'll never forget it. To us these guys were proper stars, and for weeks I'd boast about seeing them.

There wasn't much in the way of fun and diversion. There was a pool in the neighborhood that all the *pelaos* loved to go to. One day I jumped in during a practice for a swim meet. All I wanted to do was take a dip and cool off, but I didn't know how to swim and started to sink, and everyone could see I was drowning. All these people jumped in to save me.

"Hey, *pelao*, we can't have you here," the lifeguard said as they kicked me out.

So I started going to the beach to learn to swim and eventually came back and told the guy who ran the pool, "Señor Toto, I am ready to compete." He put me in the middle lane. When the starter's gun went off—*boom!*—I dove in. My main competition was a bigger guy, but I tied him.

"You can come and practice every day," Señor Toto told me. But I never got into it. I didn't want to swim. I didn't want to compete—any of that nonsense. I just wanted to show him that I could win if I wanted to.

By the time I was eleven or twelve, Toti and I had found work doing odd jobs at the Roosevelt, a hotel owned by a guy named José Manuel Gómez, who was called "Viejo"—old man. Toti had actually stayed at the hotel, living in a storage facility there, and he asked me to move in with him during that time. The hotel was popular with Americans, especially soldiers, and we worked with the maintenance crew fixing it up and doing the jobs no one else wanted to do, like throwing out the garbage. We did a good job, and Mr. Gómez took a liking to me, so I got hired to repair chairs, clean the bathrooms, paint walls, sweep floors, pick up garbage.

One day I saw a bicycle in the storeroom. "Don't even think about it," said Mr. Gómez, who'd seen me eyeing it up. "It doesn't have any brakes. If you try to ride that, you'll kill yourself."

I wasn't listening, of course. I took the bike out for a spin around eight o'clock, and I'm hurtling down this hill, scared out of my mind because all these cars are racing past me in the opposite direction. *Chuleta!* I put my feet on the ground to try to stop the bike and they got all tangled up. The bike went flying and so did I. When I finally landed, I was all banged up. My head was bleeding, my arms were all scraped, and I walked back to the hotel with that beaten-up bike and put it back, hoping Mr. Gómez would never notice that it now looked like crap. Of course he noticed, but he just laughed at me for not listening to him. "Told you so!" he kept saying. He was right, though, and I hurt for weeks afterward.

We'd also go to La Zona, the exclusive district where gringos and rich Panamanians lived, and steal mangoes. It was a restricted area—only workers with permits were allowed there—but the best mangoes were in La Zona. We were breaking the law and in danger of getting arrested for trespassing, but there were no mangoes in El Chorrillo. We'd go three at a time and cut through the fences to get the best mangoes where the other kids didn't dare go. Some kids stayed at the fence to look out for the cops while the others went for the mangoes. It was then that all the swimming practice came in handy, since we had to swim two miles to get there, load up our sacks, and then swim two miles back with the sacks floating on either side of us. Then when we got back to El Chorrillo there'd be a bunch of older kids waiting for us. They'd jump us, beat the crap out of us, and steal our mangoes. If we managed to avoid them, we'd sell the mangoes and buy food for the house. One day, I got arrested after one of these deals— not a problem, it wasn't the first time—and it turned out to be a big mistake for the cops, because when my mother came to bail me out they decided we were so poor that they gave her five dollars. Five dollars was a fortune to us, so I figured I'd better go steal some more mangoes. Then I'd get arrested again—*bam!* another five dollars, thank you very much. From then on, I got arrested every day! It was great!

We found other ways to make money. There was a place called Tiro al Blanco, a shooting range where we'd watch the gringos practice. When they'd gone, we'd collect up the lead shells while someone kept a lookout for the cops. Then we'd take them to a guy who'd weigh them and give us money for the lead. Whoever got to the shooting range first would pick up the most shells. They'd weigh a ton, but sometimes we'd walk away with six or seven dollars.

When we weren't stealing mangoes, my brother Toti and I used to deliver ice on a cart. At Christmas people would buy more ice for all the drinking they'd be doing, and I could make as much as twenty dollars, which would set us up for Christmas, too.

There was one gentleman who didn't have any money. "What can I give you instead?" he asked me.

A pair of roller skates, I told him.

"Count on it," he said.

The next day, at the Roosevelt, my brother said, "Look, this gentleman dropped a present off for you." That's how I learned to skate. I remember them so well because they were the most expensive thing I'd ever owned. I didn't grow up with things like that—my mother would say I didn't grow up with anything.

I did everything I could to help my mother, because she was looking after eight children by several different fathers. Three years after my father left, my mother met another man, Victorino Vargas. She'd fallen in love and had five children with him—Victor, Armando ("Pototo"), Chavela, Navela, and Niami. My stepfather was a musician who played guitar for a group called Sindo López. It was at a *baile típico*, a Spanish dance, that they met. My mother did find a job babysitting, but it was about forty minutes away, so she'd take some of us with her, and I'd go along with my shoeshine box and try to hustle for more money outside a restaurant while my mother took the children to a nearby park. But then she was fired—she wasn't even a very good babysitter—so I've ended up supporting my mother practically all my life, still do!

Perhaps I wouldn't have gotten into boxing at all if it hadn't been for Toti. He was a boxer before me and used to train at the old Neco de La Guardia gym. He'd have this little gym bag with him. It couldn't hold much: just the wraps, gloves, and the mouthguard. It was more like a lunch box—even his boxing shoes wouldn't fit in it. I couldn't take my eyes off it. Someday, I thought to myself, I'd like one like that. I was still only eight when one day Toti said, "Roberto, come with me."

So we show up at the gym, and Toti says, "Wait here, I'm going to the changing room." I went and sat down in the stands. And then out he comes in his boxing shorts and robe! There was a professional boxer who trained there, Adolfo Osses, a bantamweight, and he says to Toti, "You going to help me train?"

"Sure."

As I watched the trainer put the headgear on my brother, then the protective cup, I was spellbound. I wanted that.

When Toti had finished sparring I asked him how I could get all that stuff.

"Become a boxer."

So that's what I did. I went to the gym every day. But nobody wanted to work with me—I weighed eighty-four pounds. They thought I was a little *pelao*, too short and too light, and way too young. "When am I going to get a shot?" I asked Toti one day.

"You need a manager," he said.

"A manager? What's a manager?"

"A manager is somebody who could help you." But I could never find one.

Finally, when I was thirteen years old, one day I went with Toti to his weigh-in and this guy didn't show up—a 105-pounder. "I'll fight!" I told them.

Since I weighed only eighty-four pounds, the trainer put a rock in each pocket of my shorts so I could make weight. I made it to a hundred pounds exactly! Toti didn't want me to fight, because the other guy had a lot more experience—four, five, six fights—but I didn't care. I just wanted to get in the ring, even though I'd only been practicing on the bags and hadn't done any proper training yet. "I am going to beat the crap out of him," I told the trainer. I thought I would win.

And so I had my first amateur fight. I lost by decision because one of the judges was the uncle of my opponent. And the other judges were related to him, too. I actually lost my first three amateur fights. The opponents were from El Marañón gym, and they would bring the best fighters.

But at least I got three dollars out of the deal. A dollar went to my trainer, I gave a dollar fifty to my mother, and I kept fifty cents so I could go to the movies. This was the greatest thing ever, I thought—a lot better than all the crap I had to do on the streets to hustle money. No more shining shoes or selling papers for me. I was going to become a boxer.

I wanted better competition, so Toti and I would go train at El Marañón gym, which also had a basketball court. We'd show up at noon and have to wait outside for them to finish playing basketball before they'd open the doors, and then I'd train by myself. This was where I met Plomo, who would become my longtime trainer and friend. His real name was Néstor Quiñones, and he was a former amateur fighter. I went up to Plomo and told him, "I want you to be my trainer." I was still thirteen then.

"Okay," he said. "Show up at noon tomorrow." From then on, he was my trainer, and in those early days more like a father. We called him "Plomito." Plomo was special—he was tremendous at massage, for example. His brother Saúl also worked with me. Plomo taught me some things, but when you are born to box, you work things out yourself, and that's what I did. But I would stay with Plomo until his death.

Although it was Toti who got me into boxing, he wasn't my idol. That was another man, Ismael Laguna, who was Panama's greatest fighter. He was known as "El Tigre Colonense," and he had become the Panamanian featherweight champion back in 1962. When I started to learn about boxing, I realized he was the person I wanted to be. The first time I saw him fight was in 1965, when he faced Carlos Ortíz for the world lightweight title in the Estadio Nacional in Panama City. I would have been about fourteen. I traveled to the fight by jumping on a cattle truck, but I had no money to get into the stadium, so I waited. During the last three rounds they opened the gates, and you should have seen the people rushing to get in—like a swarm of ants! There were so many people charging in, it actually broke the gates. It was the end of the fourteenth round by the time I got ringside, but I was mesmerized by the whole spectacle. I remember the trainer screaming, "Hit him with a jab. Left hook! Counterpunch!" I was still a kid, but I knew then this was what I wanted to do.

Laguna won, and they gave him a giant trophy. When he came out, I followed him to his car. As they zoomed off I looked up at the sky and told myself, I am going to be just like that man—in fact, much bigger than that man. And I meant it. Because two years later I was training with him.

I was fifteen or sixteen and at my usual gym training

every day. Laguna was still world champion, yet one of the guys at the gym got hold of me and asked me to come train with the great Ismael Laguna. I wasn't overawed. It didn't worry me that he was my idol. I stayed focused in my head, knowing I had to box him. It was just another sparring session, and by then I knew what I was doing.

More important, I knew what the other guy was doing. I learned to fight inside. It worked in my favor because it reduced the distance between me and my opponent and I was able to get in powerful combinations. I had power and I was short—I wasn't going to jab anybody to death. Not a lot of guys know how to fight inside; they think it's all going-for-the-knockout bullshit. I learned ring strategy, and I taught myself how to cut off the ring. I learned those skills by myself—they're not the kinds of things someone can pass on to you. You could jab me once, but not twice. You could hit me with a left hook, but not two. You could rock me with a right, but it wouldn't happen again. I also learned, at an early age, to sense fear in my opponents. I could smell it.

Maybe it's because I never spent much time at school, but no trainer I had ever changed me. The best lesson I got was getting kicked in the head, because then I really did learn to make sure it didn't happen again. Some people think this is the hard way, but for me it was the easy way, perhaps the only way, I was going to learn.

I was comfortable in the ring now, but in my heart I was still a street fighter. Around that time, there was a guy in El Chorrillo, Chicafuerte Ruiz, a professional boxer who'd had more fights than me, and there were problems between our family and his, particularly involving my sister Marina. One day, at home, I was told what was going on, so I went around to the guy's house to sort things out. Out came Chicafuerte, the more experienced guy in the ring, and a street fight broke out, with people urging both of us on: "Chicafuerte!" "Durán! Durán!" "Chicafuerte!" I knocked the crap out of him; people were cheering like crazy. It was the first time my little brother Pototo had seen me in a street fight, although I'd already been in plenty. That was when he realized, he told me later, that I was a great fighter.

My amateur career was going quite nicely, and given my track record, I fought some very good fighters, including Catalino Alvarado, who was considered one of Panama's best boxers. Of course I beat him. I also beat Buenaventura Riasco, a top fighter from one of the top boxing clubs in Panama—I knocked him out with an uppercut. I thought I was a shoo-in to represent Panama in the Pan-American Games in 1967 in Winnipeg, Canada, and beforehand I was set to compete in a Golden Gloves qualifying tournament.

But right before the tournament, I ate something that made me sick—I'd bought something from a street vendor and they were fumigating the streets, and some of that stuff maybe got in my food. I felt really rough.

"Don't worry about it," Plomo said. "Take two Alka-Seltzers and it will go away."

I did, and at last I was ready to go. Then I drew the top two boxers in my division, who were trained by the police—

at the time, the police department in Panama had all the best boxers. But I beat the crap out of both of them, and that meant I was going to Winnipeg. Or so I thought. Then one of the colonels came up to Plomo and says he's going to send someone else.

"I won the fight!" I screamed. "*I'm* going!"

"Shut up, unless you want to end up in jail," the colonel said. That was Panama for you.

All this left me very demoralized and I didn't want to fight anymore. Screw this. All politics. Bullshit. "Plomo, if this is the way it's going to be, I'm done with it."

"Don't worry," he said. "I've got a fight for you."

"I don't want to hear."

"No, I mean a pro fight. You don't need to fight as an amateur anymore."

"How much?"

"Twenty-five dollars."

"Who do I have to kill?"

"One of the guys who didn't want to fight you as an amateur." And just like that, I turned professional.

Carlos Mendoza was from Colón and he'd already won three or four fights. He thought he was marvelous, but I'd seen him fight and knew I could handle him. But then while I was training I broke my hand hitting the heavy bag, and when we got to Colón, the doctor said I couldn't fight.

"Please let me. I need to, for my mother, to put food on the table."

So the doctor gave in. I met Plomo for a pre-fight meal of

steak and salad, which would become my ritual for the rest of my career. I won my first professional fight on February 23, 1968, a unanimous four-round decision. I was still small, only 118 pounds. I was sixteen years old.

I loved to hang out with my brother Pototo around that time. It was tough for him living at home—there were a lot of problems. When he was six, our mother gave him away to some woman, exactly the same shit she'd pulled with me. He didn't even know who she was. He cried because he didn't know the family, and eventually, a few days later, my stepfather came to get him. I'm glad I didn't find out what had happened until years afterward; I would have been very pissed off. When I was on my own, I'd pick him up and we'd go out to eat, which he really enjoyed; he knew he was getting a good meal.

We always had good times together, although one time I got really scared that I'd seriously injured him. He was recovering at home after being hit by a car, and even though he was bedridden, we ended up wrestling on the bed—we were still just kids—and he hit his head on the corner of the headboard and blacked out. Fortunately, I was able to revive him by putting alcohol under his nose.

I made sure I always brought something home for my brothers, my sisters, and my mother. I still do. Because, whatever happens, my family comes before everything.

By now, my boxing family was growing, too. My first manager was a man by the name of Alfredo Vázquez. His friends would lend him money so he could continue to be my manager and look after me. Shortly after the Mendoza fight, though, he said, "Durán, I have to tell you the truth. You're maturing as a boxer and I can't be your manager anymore. There's a gentleman named Carlos Eleta, and I'm going to have to sell my interest in you to him. It wouldn't be fair to you otherwise. I don't have the money to take you in the right direction, much less feed you properly. Every day, you're growing, and eating more."

Eleta had been impressed by me—I'd been on a preliminary card with Jesús Santamaría, one of the fighters he managed, along with a number of other good fighters in Panama, including Sammy Medina and Federico Plummer. But I had a lot more potential, Eleta knew, than any of those other guys. He asked Vázquez how much he wanted for Durán.

"I've spent, oh, a hundred and fifty dollars on him. Give me three hundred."

I was staring at them. Eleta gave Vázquez $300, and then he gave me $20. That was a lot of money then. "I will always be there for you," Eleta said. "I will always have your back." And that was that. Vázquez sold me for a miserable $300.

"We either sign a contract," Eleta told me, "or we shake hands like gentlemen."

"I'm a man of my word," I told him. "Let's shake hands." I was seventeen—I didn't have a clue about money and contracts. All I wanted to do was box, and if I could do that and put food on the table, I was happy. So we shook hands like gentlemen, but we never signed a contract. The only contract I signed was when I fought, and then I would sign it and

Eleta would cash the check. Of course, Eleta would go on to say that that $300 was the greatest investment of his life. If I had known, I would have asked for more money, but I had no idea then how much money I'd go on to make for him!

Eleta was a rich man already—the owner of a TV station, Canal Cuarto, and some distribution companies around Panama. He'd already seen one of my early fights in Colón, watched me win with courage and heart, and then he remembered who I was. It turned out we'd met previously when I was about twelve, when he'd caught me stealing coconuts from one of his trees. He told me I'd been so funny and gracious, he'd invited me to lunch instead of calling the police. I don't remember the lunch, but I do remember stealing his coconuts.

After three or four fights, Eleta told me he knew I was going to be something special, but in the beginning the relationship wasn't smooth sailing. At heart, I was still a street kid. My mother loved to go dancing at a restaurant in Chorrillo, near where we lived, and I'd usually go with her. On the way home one night, I ran into two women having an argument—one of them I knew from the restaurant—and I got between them to try to calm them down when all of a sudden some guy jumps on my back and starts choking me. Since I knew a little wrestling, I was able to flip him over, and when he stood up—*bam!*—I hit him in the face and broke his jaw. The police turned up, arrested me right away, and it turned out the guy I'd hit was a cop. I showed up in court in front of a judge who didn't like juvenile delinquents *and* was friendly with the cops, and the cop tells the judge that he went to break up the fight and I sucker punched him. I didn't say a word, so the judge sends me to jail.

But he didn't send me to juvenile jail: I found myself in Carcel Modelo, the men's jail, where there were a lot of tough guys. I got put in a cell in the corner of the prison with no toilet: I'd have to yell "Key, guard, key!" every time I needed a piss. They made us do chores like sweeping the floors and looking after the police horses. I had no shirt, because the buttons had been ripped off in that fight, and I'd given it to another prisoner to sew on new ones. I was the youngest guy in the jail.

One of the two other guys in my cell, who went by the name Taras Bulba, was a professional wrestler. He'd heard of me and knew I was a fighter with great potential. I asked him why he was in prison. The police wanted to take all of his jewelry, he told me—he wore lots of it, gold—and they'd accused him of stealing it. "I don't care," he said. "They can keep it. All I want to do is get out of here." The other one was this crazy black guy—something about him wasn't right— who looked like he wanted to start something with me. "If you touch Durán," Taras Bulba told him, "I will break both of your hands." The black guy kept being a nuisance, but thanks to Taras Bulba, he never messed with me.

Three days later, I was outside cleaning the yard when an officer came and asked me why I was in jail. I told him about the women's fight, the guy jumping me from behind, and how the guy lied in court about what had happened.

"Where are you from?"

"El Chorrillo." I told him my mother's name, my grandmother's name, and my aunt's name.

He told me he was going to look into it, but if I was lying, I'd end up doing more time. Half an hour later I was called into an office. "Okay, you're done here," said the officer. "You can go." It turns out the officer had grown up with my mother and aunt—had gone to school with them. My story checked out. But because of that nonsense, I ended up spending five days in jail.

I went to see Eleta, who told me he knew exactly what had happened but had decided not to bail me out. "I wanted to teach you a lesson so you won't do things like that." I took in what he was saying; I knew I couldn't become champion without him on my side. He had money—he was a millionaire—and I knew he'd do everything in his power to help me become champion of the world. He believed in me and I believed in him. I started calling him Papa. He wasn't my father, of course, but he was someone who looked out for me and had my best interests at heart. He became the most influential man in my life. We were in this together.

After the first fight against Mendoza, I won my next eight fights, all by knockout or TKO. Only one of them lasted more than one round. Eleta kept setting them up and I kept knocking them down.

And not just boxers—horses, too. In November 1969, I'd just fought this guy Luis Patiño from Panama City. He'd been the Panamanian bantamweight champion, but now he was getting on a bit—twenty-eight—and it was my first scheduled ten-rounder. It didn't go all the way, but it was still a hell of a fight, perhaps my toughest yet. The problem for my opponents was that I hit hard with both hands, and eventually he made a mistake. He got too close. He got a little off balance on his right foot and—*bing! bang!* tell me about it—and he didn't have a clue what had hit him. I won by TKO in the eighth. It was an extraordinary fight, and he fought only once more afterward.

After the fight, I went with my uncle Chinón to Guararé, where my family comes from, to be treated to some food, drink, and good music. Around midnight, I noticed a bunch of horses belonging to other guests tied up outside the bar. That's when this country guy comes up to me.

"Are you Durán?"

"Yes."

"I bet you a hundred you can't knock down that pony."

"No, I don't want to bet."

"How about a hundred bucks and a bottle of whiskey?"

"Are you crazy?"

But the girl I had with me starts egging me on. *"Vamos, papi."* You can do it.

"Take it," my uncle says. "I know you can knock this horse over."

I was a little drunk, but no way could I back out now. So I walk up to the pony and start looking into his long face. "Tío, where am I going to hit this animal?"

"Easy. Hit him behind the ear and he'll go down like a sack of spuds."

Boom! I knocked him down, but I didn't knock him out. Everyone is falling over laughing, the girl's kissing me, hugging me—"Oh, Papi, you knocked down the horse! You knocked down the horse!" But I'm sweating so badly, I can't concentrate, and now I realize my hand hurts like hell. One of my fingers is out of place, all dislocated, doesn't look good at all. But I was so drunk, I didn't feel a damn thing—I'd been drinking *aguardiente*, which is really strong, and slowly my whole hand, then my arm, went numb.

My uncle wanted me to go to the hospital, but we didn't, even though the bone was sticking out at an angle and looked pretty disgusting. I don't remember if it was a clinic or a house where we ended up, but the nurse told me she didn't have any anesthetic to use. I didn't care—I was still drunk. While she stitched me up I was swigging whiskey from the bottle I got from winning the bet. I didn't feel a thing. The next day, people kept asking me to tell them the whole story, which was pretty cool, and that's when I knew that the legend of Roberto Durán had been born.

My first fifteen fights were either in Panama City or Colón, and after I beat Mendoza, I knocked out the next six opponents in the first rounds. The competition got a little better in 1969, but I still won six more fights—five by TKO.

There was no one in the country who could handle me, and my reputation was spreading far and wide. That's when I knew I would have to start looking outside Panama for a decent fight. I wanted to have a shot at being world champion, and there was no way I was going to do that just by destroying everyone in Panama.

My first fight outside the country was Felipe Torres in Mexico City. He was the first man to take me the distance—ten rounds—but I still won. Then I went home again to fight in front of my fans. I was 16–0, with thirteen knockouts, when I fought Ernesto "Ñato" Marcel in May 1970 at the Gimnasio Nuevo Panamá in Panama City, with about 7,000 people in the stands, and I came in at 128 pounds. Marcel thought he was tough—he'd lost only twice in twenty-seven fights—and he was the favorite to win. I knew it was going to be my hardest fight yet and the training I did for it was brutal. I'd get up really early, at five a.m., to run, and there were times I didn't have any money for breakfast and would have to go sell newspapers before more training in the afternoon.

None of these obstacles mattered against Marcel. I hurt him in the fourth round and he started bleeding around his right eye. The ring doctor checked him out and let him continue, even though the cut was pretty deep. It was a slugfest, but I did most of the slugging, and nobody who was ringside thought the fight would go the distance. In the seventh round I tagged him hard with a right to the head and followed up with a flurry with both hands. He was in big trouble and knew it, and from that point on I dominated the fight. All he was doing was running, not wanting to get hit. The referee finally stopped it in the tenth and final round, and I won by TKO.

The trouble I did have around that fight had nothing to do with Marcel. One of Eleta's companies manufactured vitamins, and he thought it'd be a good idea if I took some to build me up a bit. I didn't know any better. I thought, If I take one, it'll make me strong. So if I take three, I'll get even stronger. I ended up just before the fight with a bad reaction, running a fever and with a lesion on my ass. For three or four days I couldn't run. "Don't give me any excuses," I remember Marcel taunting me. "I don't want to hear that you're sick, because I'm going to knock you out." I didn't tell Eleta anything, I didn't want the fight postponed.

A week before the fight, my buddy Chaparro took a look at my ass. "If you want, I can lance it and get all that crap out and you won't have a fever anymore," he said. After he'd drained out all the pus, I thought I was fine, but he said, "No, I have to take the root out," so he dug deep in there and forty-five minutes later my fever was gone, the pain was gone—everything. Next day I was able to run and tell Plomo I was fine, even though I had a hole in my ass.

In March 1971, I stopped José Acosta in the first round, and then Lloyd Marshall, and it was then I knew I was really on my way, because I started getting introduced to American celebrities. I'd met loads of famous people from Panama and South America, but now I was introduced at ringside to John F. Kennedy, Jr., the son of the dead president, who was ten years old back then. I gave him my gloves from the fight as a present.

I was fascinated by the United States of America—in love with it, even. It was a huge, strange country, but now I wanted the whole world to know who I was, and Eleta started making plans for me to fight there.

"Chuleta, vamos!" I told him. Of course I had aspirations of becoming a champion, doesn't every fighter? I wasn't dreaming big, but I wanted to win a championship so I could buy my mother a house and get her out of that shithole. That was it, nothing else. After that, I was going to retire.

It didn't work out that way.

TWO

NEW YORK,

NEW YORK

I ONCE READ A BOOK that described the skyscrapers in New York as touching the clouds. There was something magical about that city. And now I, Roberto Durán, a *pelao* from El Chorrillo, who'd spent the first four years of his career mostly fighting in Panama, was finally going to get there.

Eleta had set me up to fight Benny Huertas, a journeyman pro, in New York in September 1971, but as I flew from Panama to New York my mind wasn't on Huertas. I was looking out the window, amazed at what I was seeing, staring at Manhattan and the Empire State Building, and wondering if those skyscrapers really did touch the sky. It seems crazy now, but I really thought the plane was going to hit one of them and we'd crash.

We stayed at a hotel near Madison Square Garden, and I walked the streets in awe like a *pelao* with a bunch of new toys, so full of life. It was a little overwhelming, too, especially since I didn't speak any English, so Eleta brought in

Luis Henríquez to do the translating and order food for us while we were in camp—breakfast, lunch, dinner, he took care of pretty much everything. Everybody called him by his nickname, Flaco Bala, and he looked good at ringside in his tuxedo.

I had no interest in learning English. All I know in English is some street slang I've picked up over the years, and even now I can't write it very well. The same goes for reading, which I'm not very good at, either, just as I was never interested in business. I was a fighter: I was paid to fight. That's who I was and what I did. The rest I left to Eleta and Flaco Bala and, later, my promoter Don King. I don't even remember getting paid for my first championship fight!

And now I was in New York to fight Huertas and make people remember Roberto Durán. Manhattan was busier than any city I'd ever been in, and I knew that here I was a nobody. "The next time I come," I told myself, "they'll know who I am."

We trained outdoors in the heat of Brooklyn. People would crowd all around the ring just to watch me sparring and skipping. They brought me some sparring partners from Panama and I beat the crap out of all of them. Some days, I had to get out of the ring quickly because the canvas was so hot my feet felt like they were on fire. Thank God I didn't get any blisters. Every day I trained harder and harder. I wanted to leave my mark, and I wanted to put Panama on the map. For too long, other countries had walked all over us.

The day of the weigh-in, a Cuban woman in our camp

said, "Come on, I want to show you something," and took me for a walk. Even though it was steaming hot, everyone was running around the city like crazy. All the car horns were blaring, there were street vendors selling hot dogs—I loved it: New York was my kind of city and I wanted to make it my home. But what got me excited most of all were the different ice creams being sold on the street. (I told you I was still a street kid.) So many colors and flavors—they reminded me of home and where I came from. After the fight, and the end of the crazy regime I was on to make weight, I'd be able to have one. There was something magical about that moment, thinking back to El Chorrillo and dancing in the streets for spare change—and now walking around the greatest city in the world, about to make my debut in the United States. I'd left the hotel at lunchtime but didn't get back until five, so taken was I with the city.

"Are you crazy?" said Eleta.

"Stop worrying," I said. "When that bell rings, I'm going to knock him out, and after that I want some ice cream and some steak."

We were fighting on the undercard of the Ken Buchanan–Ismael Laguna World Boxing Association lightweight title fight. It was going to be a big night, the biggest night of my life so far, for sure. But there was one problem, and that was Huertas and his weight. He thought he was going to fight at 138–140 pounds, but the promoter switched it to 135. When I set eyes on him, he looked very muscular, clearly over the limit. Sure enough, he didn't make weight. Eleta told me a couple of pounds didn't matter. "I want you to fight this guy, Cholo. The world will see you. You are fighting in the boxing capital of the world, Madison Square Garden!"

On the night of the fight I came in wearing a shitty robe and old boxing shoes and I hadn't shaved in three days. But the important thing is that my hands were strong and fresh, and it was over before some people got to their seats. The first bell went, and the mistake Huertas made was to attack me, coming at me hard, trying to knock me out. He was big and strong and thought he could frighten me, but he opened himself up. About a minute into the fight I tagged him with a right and then a left—*bing! bing! bing!*—sixty-six seconds, he was done. He just lay down. And stayed down for a long time. Even I was surprised how quickly it was all over. Red Smith of *The New York Times* wrote that I "used only a minute or so to separate Benny Huertas from his intellect" and, in doing so, "won a rapturous following." "The undercard . . . produced one fighter of special note," *The Ring* magazine wrote, "who will have to be watched as a future lightweight champion and definite current threat. His name is Roberto Durán."

After the fight, Eleta took me to the '21' Club: "There's a party for you, Cholo," he said. I was dressed in a white suit, ready to have a good time. "Do you want some champagne? You've earned it."

"What's that?" Till then, I'd drunk only beer and whiskey.

I liked it—got a little tipsy. But I was a little down in the dumps, too, until eventually Eleta asked me what was wrong.

"Well, it's just that the Cuban lady said I'd be able to eat some ice cream in as many colors as I wanted, and now we're going back to Panama tomorrow and I haven't had any."

"That's your problem? Wait a minute!" He called someone over. Sure enough, the guy came back with a bunch of flavors. Vanilla, chocolate, mamey, guanabana, I scarfed them all. I was so stuffed, I thought I was going to explode.

A girl asked me to dance, but suddenly my stomach started churning and making embarrassing noises—*glub glub glub . . . glub glub glub.* I'd had way too much ice cream, and that champagne wasn't helping. The girl touched my stomach, and then I lost everything—and I mean *everything. Chuleta!* There was a big stain all the way down my white suit. I was panicking, walking backward, not knowing what to do. *Que cagada, coño!* Damn, that's fucked things up!

Back at the hotel I put those pants in the wash and kept rubbing and rubbing and rubbing until the chocolate-colored stain came out. And I managed to wear that same suit back to Panama!

I also went back to Panama with a new nickname, which was to stick with me for my whole career. Eleta always called me Cholo; some people called me Rocky, after Rocky Graziano, the American boxer who was famous for his knockouts, and for several fights I even wore a robe with ROCKY printed on it. But it was thanks to Plomo that I ended up with a better name. *Bam!* I'd knock somebody out with a right, and Plomo would say, "Look, I told you he hits harder with his right hand!" And then the next fight I'd knock somebody out with a left, and Plomito would say, "See—I told you so! He hits harder with his left!" So Alfonso Castillo, one of the top sportswriters in Panama, came up with the nickname "Manos de Piedra." Hands of Stone. Not *Mano* de Piedra. *Manos*— both hands. "Whoever he hits," as Castillo put it, "goes down." He began to use the nickname in his columns, on TV, and it spread like wildfire. Everyone was using it.

When we got back to Panama, Eleta moved me out of Chorrillo: there were too many gangs, too many cantinas, in the area. He got me an apartment nearer to him in Caledonia; my neighbors were a mix of middle-class and poor people. It was pretty basic: a bedroom, bathroom, living room, kitchen, and a small balcony. But Eleta had overlooked the fact that it was opposite a bar, and all the way down the street were more bars, like La Montmartre, Lo Que el Tiempo Se Llevó, Rincón Romántico—all places I soon loved to hang out in. Around the corner were even more places where they played music and I'd go to dance. New York had given me a taste of fame and the good life and I wasn't going to stop enjoying myself just because of training. Eleta would get tough with me—"Remember when I left you in prison?" he'd say—but I was a man now, twenty years old. I could do as I pleased.

There was a girl in Caledonia whose mother sold lottery tickets in the neighborhood. Her name was Felicidad and she was then fourteen years old and still in school. She'd get out of class at four in the afternoon and walk home, and her mother would give her the money she'd earned from lottery tickets to go get food for her brothers and sisters. There were six of them in the family, but her mother was still able to put food on the table for them every day.

Felicidad didn't like me at first; her cousin Ana was in love with me, but Felicidad would tell her not to pay me any attention, because she thought I was a womanizer, that I had too many girlfriends and liked to party too much. But one day I saw Felicidad walking down the street and called out, "Whoa, slow down, blondie! You're going like a train!" And then I asked her out. "Fulita, let me take you out to dinner tomorrow." She said yes, though she was worried because her mother was very strict. She told me to meet her at the Don Bosco church: tomorrow, January 31, was the day of Saint John Bosco.

The next day, then, we went to a restaurant, and then on to the Lux Theater for a movie about killer rats, and then another movie. Fulita had permission to stay out only until seven or she would be punished, and by now it was very close to her curfew. I persuaded her to forget about it and come dancing at the Morocco bar. After that, we went to a hotel, where we could be alone, and by the time we left there, it was eleven at night . . .

We had a great time together, but Fulita was terrified and thought her mother would kill her. We got back to her front door and I could see her mother waiting at the window for her to show up, but she didn't see us. Fula was too scared to go in.

"Fula, I'll take you back to my place tonight and tomorrow

I'll talk to your mother." Two days passed and still I hadn't had that talk with her mother, who was going crazy and looking for her all over the place, in hospitals, even the morgue to see if she had been killed.

My sparring partner Chico found Fula's mother crying on the street. "Señora, I will tell you. She is with Roberto Durán. Please don't hit her." She came to my apartment, screaming at Fula, "You are coming home!"

"No, I'm staying with him!"

After half an hour, her mother and father came back with the police, who took us both to the station house. They didn't arrest me, but they told Fula she had to go back to her parents', as she was still a minor. They locked her in the house—all because she'd wanted to go out and have some fun.

Earlier in the week I'd bought her a turquoise bracelet, and now she asked her cousin Ana to give me her phone number so we could arrange a meeting for her to give it back to me. But this was a ruse to keep seeing me, and once she was allowed to leave the house again, we met secretly for three months.

Eventually, her mother gave up trying to prevent us from seeing each other; she knew there was nothing she could do to stop it. Finally, very reluctantly, her parents decided that if that was the life she wanted, she could go stay with me. Of course, within six months her parents and I were best friends. They loved me as much as they loved her, because they saw that I was a good man who treated their daughter like a queen. We wouldn't marry until fourteen years after we met, but since those days we have been inseparable.

There would be other important changes in my life around this time. Back in September 1970, Scotland's Ken Buchanan had traveled to Puerto Rico to meet Ismael Laguna from Panama for the world lightweight championship. A lot of people, including me, thought Laguna would win, especially because of the climate. We didn't think Buchanan would be able to deal with the heat. But he beat Laguna in a fifteen-round decision. He beat my idol, the idol of all of Panama! Laguna was no longer the fighter he had been. I got right on Eleta. "I want you to get me a fight with Ken Buchanan. I'll beat him."

So in March 1972, I had my last fight before I got my opportunity to challenge the world title, against Francisco "Panchito" Muñoz in Panama City. Then it would be on to New York and Ken Buchanan for the WBA lightweight title at Madison Square Garden on June 26. And for this, Eleta recruited two legends of the sport to work my corner.

Ray Arcel, especially, had trained some of the best— Henry Armstrong, Kid Gavilan, Benny Leonard, a bunch of others. Now Eleta, who knew him well, had convinced him to come out of retirement to work with me. Freddie Brown, too, had a great reputation, working as a cuts man or trainer with guys like Floyd Patterson and Rocky Marciano—he'd worked Marciano's corner throughout his undefeated career. "I'm going to make you world champion," said Eleta, "but you've got to go and train in New York. I've already talked to him."

"Señor Eleta, I'm not going to New York unless I go with Plomo," I replied. "Nobody is going to take Plomo away from me. I was born with Plomo, I grew up with Plomo, and I'll die with Plomo."

"Don't worry, Cholo, no one's going to take Plomo away from you. But these two gentlemen, who are legends in the sport, are going to join him."

Arcel was impressed when he met me. He thought I could be another Jack Dempsey; he could see I was street-smart— if you have that, you can do anything in the ring. He and Brown had four basics they wanted every fighter to follow:

> The left is as important as the right.
> Boxing is the art of hitting and not getting
> hurt.
> It's not how hard you hit a man but where you
> hit him.
> The speed with which you cut up an opponent
> is directly related to how efficiently you cut
> off the ring.

I thought I knew it all in boxing, but now these guys taught me a lot of tricks I went on to use in the ring. I was convinced it was only a matter of time before I became famous in boxing and made them even more famous. I knew now what I had to do and it wasn't just about beating Buchanan, which I knew I could do with my eyes shut. What was more important was the *way* I beat him. I had to use the fight to show the world I was the greatest boxer around. And now these two legends would join me and help me prepare for the greatest challenge of my young career.

The training was brutal with those guys, even though Eleta had made things easier by paying for my apartment. I still ran very early in the morning, around five o'clock, rested, had breakfast at ten, then trained in the afternoon from two onward. First I'd shadowbox to warm up, then work the speed bag for three or four rounds. After that, I hit the heavy bag—five minutes, three minutes, it varied. Then fifteen minutes of rope, then physical conditioning exercises for fifteen minutes. I'd spar three or four rounds. Sometimes Brown would have me go as many as seven rounds, at three minutes each.

WHEN WE MADE THE FIGHT, I had another request for Eleta: bring Chaflán. Chaflán was always asking me for a favor; this time it was, "Take me to New York." He'd never thought he would leave Panama, but thanks to a man of influence like Carlos Eleta he was able to get a visa, because you don't get a visa just like that.

Chaflán came to stay in the same hotel with me in New York, and would come watch me training at Grossinger's gym. But he got a bit out of control. He loved New York nightlife, and once when I went to pick him up at the hotel he wasn't there. I found him in a bar, dancing to get tips from customers. I told him if the gringos found out, they would send him back to Panama, and that was the end of babysitting Chaflán. It was the only fight he came to. I kept my promise to bring him to one of my fights.

I had other things to worry about—I had a fight to win. Buchanan saw me as just a kid from Panama, a nobody, and must have thought he was in for an easy time. He sat next to me at a press conference, having some bread and butter and a Coke, while behind us they were showing a clip of me beating Hiroshi Kobayashi in October 1971. A reporter asked him if he'd seen that fight and he said no, and added that I was too slow for him. I laughed. This fool doesn't know the shitstorm that's going to come down on him, I thought to myself.

Buchanan disrespected me, but what really made me mad was that he said I was a lucky boy because I'd never had to fight my way up, step by step, the way he had. But he didn't know Roberto Durán. I was raised in the streets, had to hustle for food every day. I've been fighting every single day of my life since I was a *pelao*. "Ever since I was a little kid I felt nobody could beat me," I told reporters. "I have no respect for him. I'm undefeated—he should respect that."

I trained hard, worked on my speed. I didn't train as if I was going to fight fifteen rounds, I trained as if I was going to fight twenty-five rounds. Instead of sparring three-minute rounds, I did four and a half minutes.

The night of the fight, Arcel looked straight at me. "I suppose you won't go back to Panama if you lose tonight."

"If I lose," I told him, "I'll kill myself."

I didn't care that I was the two-to-one underdog. I knew all my hard training had given me twice the speed Buchanan had. I was very confident. At the weigh-in I sneered at him, trying to make eye contact, knowing he'd be afraid of me. On the night of the fight I felt inspired the moment I left the dressing room: I could feel that I had it in me to take this guy down. Buchanan came out serenaded by bagpipes; I came out with a taste of my country's *sabor*: a marimba band with flamenco dancers.

I started strong and knocked him down in the first round with a sharp left to the head, even though some people thought it was a slip. But I give him credit for being strong the whole fight—another fighter would have been knocked out in four or five rounds, but he took a lot of punishment.

After the third round, the Americans tried to put me at a disadvantage when the boxing commissioner asked Flaco Bala, my translator, to leave my corner—only three handlers were allowed in each corner. Arcel and I were still getting to know each other, and I didn't speak English, he didn't speak Spanish. So now all Arcel could do was use simple words like "Jab, jab, jab" and "Punch, punch, punch." But I knew what I had to do. I was born a boxer and I was in my element—this was going to be my day and I was going to let nothing get in the way.

My right was beating his left lead consistently, and I would feint with the right and hook with the left while I kept my right hand in his face. His main weapon, the jab that had caused such problems for Laguna, was nothing. He was in so much trouble that in the middle of the fight he had to spit out his mouthguard so he could breathe.

Finally, at the end of the thirteenth round, I had him against the ropes. He took a shot to the rib cage and went down. When he returned to his corner, he couldn't continue fighting. He said I had hit him with my right hand in the nuts after the bell, but the referee, Johnny LoBianco, said it was a fair blow. He said the punch was "in the abdomen, not any lower." It was more that I was smaller and he was taller.

The truth is that he just couldn't take it anymore. At any minute I thought the referee was going to stop the fight. Buchanan was fast, but I was faster, and I wanted it more—to win the title and bring it back to my idol, Ismael Laguna.

What is true is that if Ray Arcel and Freddie Brown hadn't been in my corner, I wouldn't have become world champion. Because, as I understand it, they knew a number of the judges and the referee for that fight. I don't know how things would have gone if it had just been Plomo in my corner, because of our limited English. I remember Arcel asking the referee in English, "What are you going to do now?"

But Buchanan said I should have been disqualified—for what, hitting him too much?—and of course there were people making excuses for him, including the American journalists. Red Smith of *The New York Times* wrote that LoBianco had to award the fight to me, since in boxing "anything short of pulling a knife is regarded indulgently."

I was disappointed because I didn't want there to be doubt

in anyone's mind that I was the world champion. What no one could dispute was that I'd done it at the age of just twenty-one. The point of boxing is fighting for world titles, so perhaps that night is my first great memory. There weren't as many boxing associations back then as there are today—nine or ten these days, but only three at that time. You had to work hard to get there, fight the best—not like nowadays. I earned that title with my fists.

Felicidad had stayed in Panama for the fight, and when I called her afterward, she told me everyone had taken to the streets. It was a new world for her—she had never seen anything so extraordinary. Now I was getting a lot of stuff for winning. Eleta had promised me a car if I won. Before the fight, I'd been to visit the Panamanian ambassador and he'd said, "If you become world champion, I will have an outfit made for you, whatever you want." A gentleman who worked on the Avenue of the Americas offered to make me a white suit, and it cost some $200.

General Omar Torrijos, Panama's military ruler, sent his plane, stocked with champagne, to bring me back, and I walked off that plane in that suit and a white Panama hat—there are lots of pictures of me celebrating in that suit and hat—into mayhem. At the airport I was completely mobbed: there must have been several thousand people, although it felt like half the country had turned out. They had yellow tape to keep the crowds back, but when they saw me they rushed through it, screaming, "Durán! Durán!" My wife still gets goose bumps telling the story.

General Torrijos had laid on a government limo to take us to Via España for a parade. You couldn't walk anywhere in the city because people were out on the streets, cheering, crying, fainting. They weren't used to something so spectacular. Ismael Laguna had been Panama's hero, and my hero and inspiration, and now one of the first things I did was take the championship belt to him and say, "Here—this is yours." But Laguna didn't want it: "I'm happy enough that you won," he said. Now this worship was on another level. Panama had a new hero. Rich or poor, people loved Durán.

After the parade, Fula and I went to the presidential residence to drink champagne and eat with General Torrijos. The president noticed I was sweating and gave me one of his shirts. I told him I was tired and I'd better get home. "No," he said, "you're staying here tonight. I'm going to my private residence and you can be president for a day." So that's where Felicidad and I stayed.

There were tears of pain around this time, too. Fula hadn't come with me to the Buchanan fight because she was pregnant, and one evening, while I was in New York, my mother accidentally took a chair out from under Fula as she went to sit down, and she landed in a heap on the floor. Later that evening when they all went out to see a Bruce Lee movie, Fula felt blood trickling down her legs. She was a month and a half pregnant and she lost the baby.

She didn't tell me while I was training, so of course I brought a cuddly toy back from New York for her, thinking we were going to celebrate the birth of our first child. That's when she finally told me what had happened. "If that's God's plan," I told her, "we have to accept it." Seven months later, she was pregnant with Roberto Jr., known as Chavo. We were building a life together.

The reaction to my victory was immediate and huge. It started at the top with Torrijos, of course. The Panamanian government was very active in promoting all of the country's great fighters, starting with me. I wasn't the only champion: Alfonso "Peppermint" Frazer had won the WBA junior welterweight title in March 1972. And there were two other very good fighters, Enrique Pinder and Ñato Marcel, a featherweight contender. In 1970, Torrijos had set up the National Institute of Culture and Sports, mostly to promote boxing, and from then on whenever one of us fought outside Panama, the government would help pay the cost of showing the fight nationally on live TV. That's what they did for the Buchanan fight. Torrijos even promised a lifelong monthly pension of $300 for every Panamanian boxer who became a world champion. Ismael Laguna was the first, of course. Then came Frazer. I'd be next.

Winning the world championship only made my friendship with the general stronger. I'd known him since I lived in El Chorrillo, when he was still a lieutenant in the Panamanian Army living close by, and his kids Martín and Dumas also wanted to practice boxing. His job meant he couldn't take them to training, so Plomo got me to pick them up—I was twelve years older than Martín—take them to the gym to train, and then bring them back home. I was given five dollars for the week to cover their meals, and by the weekend I had a couple of bucks to give back, saying, "Señor Torrijos, here's what's left."

"You're a decent *pelao*," Torrijos said. "I'd like you to do this every week."

The kids kept growing, and then one day Martín Torrijos, the general's own son, announced that he was going to the United States to study at a military academy, and later at Texas A&M. In 2004, he became president of Panama, after winning the election with the support of singer and politician Rubén Blades—who'd also become my friend—and everyone from the old days started circling around him looking for favors, but we never asked anything from him. After the Buchanan victory, though, a friend of mine kept bugging me to ask General Torrijos for a car. So I did. I was at his office, and he calls up a colonel and yells over the phone, "Go get Durán a car!" I'd asked for a Volkswagen—that was all I wanted—but the colonel got me a luxury model with all the extras. And that's the only thing I ever asked for.

The world had certainly changed for me and Felicidad, but we tried to keep things simple. We stayed in the same apartment because I had an endorsement deal with the Super Malta beverage company and it paid the rent, which was only $125 a month, fully furnished. But eventually Eleta would buy me a house in El Cangrejo, a neighborhood with palm trees and an outdoor courtyard. It was a long, long way from where I had come from. El Cangrejo, literally "the crab"; it's called that because its streets are spread out like a crab's claws.

In the 1950s it was a Jewish neighborhood, and one of the most modern and fancy in Panama. It was a twenty-minute ride from El Chorrillo, close enough for me to go back and see my old friends.

The son of the lady who lived in the upstairs apartment across from our new house happened to be Martín Torrijos, whom I hadn't seen since I used to take him to the gym. It turned out that the general, who was now the most powerful person in the country, had had an affair with this woman and Martín was the result—in fact, he was the only one of his sons who did look like him. It was as though his head had been cut off and given to Martín, or the other way around. Because his mother was terrified that something would happen to him, the only place she would let him go was our house, so he'd come and eat with us, even do his homework. I had a pool installed, and he'd go for a swim while Felicidad was cooking for him, and then he'd be back home in time for bed.

Sometimes the general would arrive at one, two in the morning with all his bodyguards, and because he trusted us he'd get them to leave his guns at our house. "How are you doing, son?" he'd say to me. "Is everything okay? I'm going upstairs—do you have any whiskey?"

"Yes, Chivas Regal."

He'd go upstairs for some you-know-what, and I'd sit drinking whiskey with his bodyguards. He'd drop by twice a week, so we got to know him pretty well. He'd come back down around five or six a.m., asking for whiskey. The woman upstairs would eventually be godmother to one of my daughters.

Who would ever have imagined all this back in the days when I was training his kids? The general never thought I was going to be champion of the world, and I never thought he'd end up a general of the Republic of Panama. And I never, ever thought that later young Martín would grow up to become president of the Republic of Panama. But these are the kinds of things that can happen in life.

The Volkswagen I got from the general after beating Buchanan soon got me into bad trouble. I was in love with a woman named Silvia from Puerto Armuelles in Chiriquí province, and one day I was on my way to see her in my new car. The trip took us up into the hills, and just as we were approaching David, a town way out in the countryside, it started to pour. The road turned to mud and I couldn't see shit. I tried to slow down as we hit a bend, and I thought I'd crossed over into another lane. Suddenly a car flashed its lights in front of me. *Bam!* I slammed on the brakes, the car spun around, and now we were hurtling downhill. The car crashed into a big tree trunk, and that's what saved me from dying. I busted my right elbow, and my lip was a real mess. The hitchhiker I'd picked up along the way had a head injury.

It was still pouring down rain as we walked back up the hill to get help, and by that time, I was bleeding badly from my mouth and arm. Plodding up, up, uphill in that downpour. When we finally reached the top, the rain stopped, a car came out of nowhere, and the driver recognized me and stopped.

He gave us a ride to the hospital in San Félix, but I was

getting more and more worried about how I was going to explain this to Felicidad. And I wasn't the only nervous one. The doctor who was stitching me up, his hands were shaking. "Why are you trembling?" I asked him.

"Durán, I'm afraid you're going to die here."

"Doctor, if I didn't die out on the hill, I'm not going to die here." I was still forty minutes away from David, where there were a bunch of people waiting for me, and I told the doctor I had to go. He tried to stop me, but there was nothing he could do.

When I got there, we started drinking and met a few girls, and apart from the pain where they stitched me up, it was a great night. Word got out about the accident and lots of fans came by to see me—even the local chief of police, an old friend, came by to wish me well. When the bars closed, we kept partying at the Hotel Nacional, and the next day we went on to Puerto Armuelles. When I got back to Panama City, my arm still bandaged up, I had to explain it all to Fula. She was not happy.

But that was nothing compared to my horror when I found out that Eleta had signed me up to fight Esteban de Jesús. He was considered one of the top lightweights in the world, with twenty-seven knockouts—ten in the first round. Eleta and General Torrijos wanted me to make my first title defense in Panama, and when a deal could not be worked out, they'd set up this non-title fight in New York. "Why, Eleta?" I asked him. "My mouth's all swollen. My elbow's busted."

"I've signed the contract," he said. "You've got to fight."

The fight was set for November 17, 1972. It was time to get ready for my return to Madison Square Garden.

Even though the pain affected my workload, I went into training. I ended up weighing five pounds more than for the fight against Buchanan (137½). De Jesús weighed 138. The odds were stacked against me from the get-go. Ten thousand people and every one of them Puerto Rican. But I was Durán: I'd come through hell to get here—I could deal with anything.

First round, inside a minute—*boom!*—he catches me with a left hook and dumps me on my ass for the first time in my professional career. The referee, Arthur Mercante, starts counting, "One, two, three . . ." I get up right away, shake my head, and smile.

Now I rallied. I was bleeding through my mouth—they'd taken the stitches out, but it was still swollen. My elbow still hurt. I hurt him in the eighth with a right. If I hadn't had that car crash, I would have put him on his knees. The only thing he did was knock me down. I knew I'd won that fight, but they gave it to him by unanimous decision. In thirty-two fights it was the first time I had lost, and after the post-match press conference, which I don't remember much about, I went back to my hotel room, cried, beat my fists against the wall, and promised myself I would never lose again. I told Eleta I wanted revenge, and they had to give it to me. But I'd have to wait awhile: it would be fifteen months before I faced him again.

I was pissed that I lost. I got a lot more pissed when the

Panamanian press turned on me for the first time in my career, questioning whether I'd trained properly and suggesting that I partied too much. That was bullshit, but they loved to dump on me when I was down. This would be only the first time.

Two months later, I knocked out Jimmy Robertson in the fifth round in Panama City to retain my WBA lightweight title. It was in front of a capacity crowd of 18,000 people at the Gimnasio Nuevo. They saw a good show, and for good measure, I took out a couple of his teeth with a right cross in the fifth round.

After that, we went to Los Angeles for two fights, against Juan Medina and Javier Ayala. The first one was scheduled with Medina on February 22, 1973. Fula came with me, but only for the first fight—this pregnancy with Chavo was so difficult, she was vomiting constantly. She'd feel so dizzy that eventually she told Señor Eleta she would make me worry too much if she stayed, and so she flew back to Panama and went straight to the hospital for a month. But before she left, she was at the gym the day I finally met my father.

I'm doing heavy-bag work when one of my handlers comes up and says: "Durán, I'd like you to meet your family." First I was introduced to a man and a woman who said they were my aunt—my father's sister—and uncle—her husband—and that my father wanted to come see me. I had my father's nose, they told me: a big nose (which I've since had cosmetic surgery on). We arranged for me to meet him at the gym the next day.

I was more nervous than I thought I would be. After all, I hadn't seen him since I was one and a half—why should I care about him? Eleta introduced us.

"How do I know you're my father?" I said. "Prove it."

"I know your uncle Moisés, your uncle Chinón, your grandmother . . ."

When he described to me where my mother used to live, I knew then he was my dad. He took me to his house to meet the rest of the family, and after that we came back to my hotel and talked some more. It hadn't been his idea to leave when I was only eighteen months old, he said; he'd been posted from Panama to Arkansas. He'd been born in Arizona, of Mexican heritage, and had stayed in the army until he was thirty-nine. He'd also served in Vietnam. This was all very interesting, but it meant nothing to me. I just kept thinking he was making excuses for abandoning us.

In the early seventies, he said, he'd picked up a Mexican boxing magazine that had me listed as the number 6 contender in the lightweight division. That had made him feel proud, he said. But perhaps he didn't feel anything more, either, because we quickly ran out of things to say.

The one person I immediately bonded with was my grandmother, Estelle, my father's mother. My father had named me Roberto after his brother, and she looked at me and said: "This is Roberto Durán. This is my blood." She was eighty-five and a Cherokee Indian, and she used to put her long hair up in braids. She had heard about me but, until I came to Los Angeles, hadn't been able to make contact. "This is my grandson!" she'd say proudly, and she wanted to enjoy her final years with me.

From then on, my grandmother and my dad started coming to my fights—and of course, they wanted the best hotels and tickets for everyone. I went along with it—I was making good money and had no reason not to. My dad came to three or four fights, then got bored and stopped coming. After that, I never saw him again. But my grandmother kept coming, no matter where they were, almost until she passed away. She was my biggest fan. "I am not leaving my grandson behind," she would say. A good, good lady. I adored her.

Eventually, so many years after the last time I had seen my father, one of my relatives in Los Angeles called to say that he was doing very poorly and it was his wish to be taken off life support. They asked me what I thought. I didn't feel anything at all. If they want to kill my father, that's fine, I thought, but I'm not going to do it. His death was not going to be on my conscience. They had lived with him all their lives, let them make that decision. A week later I got a call saying that he'd died. I felt no emotion. I respected him as my father, but as for love, remember that a child who grows up in poverty, who has no father, only a mother, is always going to think, Why did my dad abandon me? All he did was make me, see me, and then leave me. That's all. May he rest in peace.

IN THE RING, I was still dominating like a champion. I was killing everybody I fought since losing to de Jesús, winning ten fights in a row, eight by knockout, and everyone knew it. And finally, in March 1974, I got to fight de Jesús again. Forget the rest, this was the one I wanted—the chance to avenge that defeat, the fight I knew I would have won if it hadn't been for the car crash. De Jesús had won eight straight fights, with three knockouts, including Ray Lampkin twice, Johnny Gant, and Alfonso "Peppermint" Frazer, the former champion from Panama. I didn't give a shit about any of that. He wasn't going to beat me. And the boxing people knew it, too. I was a two-to-one favorite.

This time, he would have to face me in Panama, in the 18,000-seat Gimnasio Nuevo. The gross was expected to be $400,000, one of the largest gates in the history of boxing in the country. I was going to make $125,000, with de Jesús guaranteed $40,000. There was worldwide interest in it—it was going to be televised live in the United States, Venezuela, Puerto Rico, and some countries in Europe. Ringside seats were going for $100, which was big money in those days.

Before the fight, de Jesús' manager tried to come up with excuses for losing before I'd even thrown the first punch. De Jesús had suffered a cut lip while training, he said—the fight might have to be postponed. It all got resolved at the last minute, and we were going to have our fight on my home turf.

Then, what do you know, at the beginning of the first round, about ninety seconds into the fight—*boom!*—he hits me with the same hook that dropped me in the first fight! *Chuleta!* Same fucking hook! I got up immediately and took a standing eight count. He thought I was groggy. My fans were worried, too, jumping out of their seats, screaming for me to get up. But I wasn't in any trouble. I went over to my corner, shook my head, and told them I was fine. I got up and started working him over. Up and down. All over the place. I worked him inside and kept pounding him. It was hot as hell in that stadium, which was better for me because I'd trained in that kind of heat all my life. It wasn't so good for him, and I sensed his strength ebbing as the rounds went by. He was mine and I just needed to finish him off.

I took him down with a five-punch combination in the seventh round. I knew he was done then, and I finished him off in the eleventh round with a left hook to the head, a shot to the body, and another right cross to the head.

There it was: revenge, and my thirty-fifth knockout in forty-two fights. It was a great night for me, beating him like that in front of my people, and it was a good night for me, too, with the money. That $125,000 was the biggest purse of my career to that point, and right away Eleta started talking about a potential rematch with Buchanan, maybe in Canada. I wasn't bothered. Whichever guy Eleta found who was brave enough to fight me, I was going to kill him.

After beating de Jesús, I went back to my house, where my mother-in-law threw a party for me, and we were up until five in the morning, drinking and partying. But around seven, a bunch of cops knocked on the door. I thought I was dreaming. They just knocked harder and harder until they eventually got me out of bed, hungover as hell. "Señor Torrijos wants you to go to Cuba," one of the police captains told me.

"Cuba? I haven't even been paid for the fight yet."

"You'll get paid when you get back." The cops threw me in the shower, got me dressed, and put me on the presidential plane to Cuba.

It all happened so quickly, I'd forgotten to take my passport, and before I knew it we'd landed in Cuba to be greeted by this big Cuban guy with an attitude. "Hey, Chico, where's your passport? You need your passport or we'll arrest you."

"I don't give a shit"—I really didn't. All I wanted to do was go back to bed.

Finally, they took me to this barracks and there was Torrijos, sitting all alone at a long table. "My son!" he said, offering me a glass of whiskey I definitely didn't want. "I want to introduce you to Castro. You'll like him—he's a boxing fan like me. We've got a lot in common."

In due course we ended up at this white castle, which looked like a museum but was actually Fidel Castro's presidential residence. There I was shown his memorabilia, including some of the weapons he'd used when he came down from the mountains during the revolution.

And then there was Castro, sitting next to Torrijos. Torrijos jumped up and shouted out for everyone to hear, "Durán, I would like you to meet Fidel!" I turned my back on him to put my drink down, which apparently you're not supposed to do—another person would have shit in his pants and dropped his drink—but me, I turned my back on him and then I sized him up. Castro looked at me quizzically, cigar in mouth, as though he was thinking, No one has ever done that to me. Eventually, he shook my hand and we talked for a while.

That night we went to a baseball stadium to see the Cuban heavyweight Teófilo Stevenson. They had seats for me at the front, but I went to the back, because if there was a shooting, the generals and their group were the ones who were going to get hit. This is typical of me—I always think the worst. But a henchman came over and said, "The Comandante wants you to sit with him," so reluctantly I went and sat next to Castro.

There had always been discussion of how Stevenson would fare against Muhammad Ali. He'd been considered the world's premier amateur heavyweight after winning a gold medal in the Munich Olympics, but somehow he'd never managed to take the way Ali had. Tonight he was fighting some chump who weighed 147 pounds; somehow the guy was giving the great Olympian, who weighed close to 200 pounds, a beating through the first three rounds. And then all of a sudden the *pelao* seemed to get tired. Something wasn't right.

Midway through the third round, Castro turns to me, chomping on his cigar, and addresses me as a brother: "*Oye, consorte*, Cassius Clay and Stevenson—how do you see it going?"

"*Lo mata, jefe. Lo mata.*" He'll kill him, chief. He'll kill him.

"You mean Stevenson kills Cassius Clay?"

"*No, jefe.* Cassius Clay kills Stevenson."

He looks at me again, chomping on his cigar.

"Sir, do you know that Clay is on the way down?"

"No, sir. You're wrong. In his whole life Stevenson has never fought fifteen rounds. He's only fought three- and four-rounders in the amateurs. And Ali can take a lot of shots—Stevenson won't be able to knock him out. Ali has too much experience for him. Next to Ali, Stevenson looks like a little kid."

"*Oye, consorte,* how can you say that?" Fidel was amazed I hadn't picked his guy. But I was a hundred percent right. Ali would have killed Stevenson if they'd ever fought.

When I got back to Florida, where I was training at the time in Miami Beach, all the Cuban journalists descended on me, thinking I was buddy-buddy with Fidel. I understood how close Miami was to Cuba and how many Cuban exiles were there—and everywhere I went they asked me what it was like back there now and how a *pelao* like me could end up sitting next to Castro. I tried telling them what had happened, but no one believed me!

To be honest, I couldn't care less about politics or politicians—as far as I'm concerned, each is as bad as the other. So I told them: Whoever comes from Cuba to Panama, I am friends with them. Whoever comes from Cuba to Miami, I am friends with them. If Castro is a Communist, that's his problem. I live my life.

As it happened, my greatest friend was a Cuban: Victor del Corral, owner of Victor's Café in Manhattan. He was like a father to me—a real father—and I loved him like the devil.

And he treated me like his son, since he'd never had one of his own, only a daughter. I got to know him when I began fighting in New York, as I was always on the lookout for Latin food. It was just before I fought Huertas in 1971 that we first went to Victor's Café, and my translator Flaco Bala introduced me to Victor: "He is going to be world champion one day."

"Have whatever you want," Victor said. "On us."

His restaurant was on Seventy-first and Columbus Avenue, and since it opened in 1963 had become very famous. It was always packed with New Yorkers, people from Latin countries, and celebrities—stars like Barbra Streisand, Liza Minnelli, and Michael Douglas—but I was always treated as a favorite. Every time I was in New York to fight, we'd work out at the gym until we were half dead and then head to Victor's place. The bond between us lasted for the rest of our lives. Through good times and bad, he never deserted me. I can't say that about everyone.

THREE

THE

LION

KING

My love of boxing was second only to my other passion—music. Specifically, *música típica* from Panama, and salsa music. I was a big fan of Rubén Blades. We'd met as teenagers when he was in a group called Bush y Sus Magníficos and playing at some club in Panama City—a mutual friend introduced us. I told him I loved music and would have been a singer if I could. He laughed and told me I sang as badly as he boxed, and he wasn't wrong.

The biggest influence on my musical life, though, was my brother Pototo. From when he was a kid, he'd be at clubs all night singing and I'd be waiting for him outside after he got paid in case something happened, like a fight. It was tricky: I wanted to watch his back, but I didn't want to get arrested. Then we'd go out to eat, before bringing the money back for our mother. Plomo's brother was a conga player: he'd shown Pototo how to play the congas, and from then on Pototo was the star. The idea of the band came from a friend who'd just been released from jail and wanted to get an orchestra together and wondered if I could help him financially. Sure, I told him, on the condition that my brother plays congas. "And if he's no good," I said, "then, fine, he's gone."

And so we formed an orchestra, which also included one of my best friends, Marcos Guerrero, an excellent musician. I'd known him since we were *pelaos* growing up in El Chorrillo, and although we didn't hang out together a lot, I'd occasionally run into him after he got involved in music and playing congas and percussion in local bands. It would be the start of a lifelong friendship.

We named the group Los Mamalucos, Panamanian slang for "overalls." I bought all the instruments—they cost $40,000, but it was worth it—we started practicing, and we added real quality by bringing in Camilo Azuquita, a singer who was very well known in Panama. We recorded an LP, *Dos Campeones*, Two Champions, which was well received and sold strongly. In 1975, I'd record my first album with Pototo's other salsa band, doing vocals on several songs.

Between my fights, we toured as much as we could—to Colombia, then back to New York, where I introduced the band to Victor—but the problem was, the guy, who'd been released from jail, was keeping most of the money for himself and giving the little that was left to the musicians. I didn't care about the money because I was getting loaded from my fights, but it still made me mad, so I took the instruments away for a while. That seemed to do the trick.

My trouble was that I was having too much fun, and by 1974 it was all too much of a distraction from training. I was twenty-five, and 135 pounds was a hard weight for me to hold as world champion with all the music and the partying. I was going to have to quit the music or I was going to have to find another way to keep my weight down, which was a drag. I didn't have time to be world champion at 135 pounds!

Despite these concerns, my boxing career was still going well, as I expected. After de Jesús, I breezed through five more fights, including my fifth defense of my WBA light-weight title against Masataka Takayama, knocking him out in the first round in San José, Costa Rica, in December 1974. I knew I had him even before we fought—it was easy, perhaps too easy. Two rights, he went down for the first time. Another right—*boom!*—he went down again. And then I finished him with a couple of hooks and another right to the head. It was over in a hundred seconds, after which I got right back to the good life. Takayama said I hit him without mercy, that I hurt him, and that he had no chance against all my punches. He was right on all counts.

That was easy. Ray Lampkin was not. He was my second opponent of 1975—this time, in March—as I defended my WBA lightweight title in Panama City. I loved fighting there, of course, even though when I fought outside Panama, ABC would show the fights in my country—they brought in their satellite trucks and stayed at the Panama Hilton. It was all so new and exciting for my family.

Lampkin coming from the United States to meet me on my home turf would give me an immediate advantage. He was a good prospect, coming in with a 29–3–1 record that included twelve knockouts. He had also lost to de Jesús twice, both in twelve rounds, and had won six straight fights since the last defeat by him, and also held the North American Boxing Federation lightweight title. But then he had to face me, at home, in front of my people, in an outdoor arena, hot and humid—all things that worked in my favor, so I didn't lose too much sleep over it.

Unfortunately, I realized too late that I was having a hard time making the weight. I was getting too big, and now that I was world champion and there were so many distractions, it was hard for me to stay disciplined. *Cerveza. Comida.* Beer. Food. With a week to go, I could still do it, but it was far from ideal: losing that much weight in such a short period of time takes it out of you. By the time the fight came around, I was ready, but I didn't know what the cost would be.

Lampkin thought he could beat me with his speed by throwing me off my timing. In the first round he stayed on the outside, knowing that if he got too close I would land one of my trademark hooks. He managed to connect with some rights to the body in the second, but he never hurt me, and I got some of my own shots in, as the people of Panama kept hollering and cheering me on. His punches weren't hurting me, and even though my preparation had not been ideal, I still felt invincible.

Minute by minute I kept the pressure on him and continued attacking. He did make it to the twelfth round, which made him the longest-lasting challenger of my career till then, so good for him, but he had a black eye and didn't seem up for the fight. I knew he wouldn't go the distance. Less than thirty seconds into the fourteenth round, I caught him with a hook flush on his jaw—*bam!* I fooled him with a flash of my hands and he covered up, thinking I was going to hit him with a right, but I tagged him with a left—Manos de Piedra right there. I knocked him out and he fell back and his head hit the canvas. He wouldn't be getting up anytime soon.

It was when I went back to my corner, arms over my head for the crowd, who were singing my name, that I realized I'd hurt him badly. They carried him out on a stretcher, and he was having convulsions before he had even left ringside. The doctors had to give him oxygen in the dressing room. He was out for over an hour and ended up in the hospital for five days. His left leg was temporarily paralyzed and he was close to death. He was lucky I wasn't in the best shape for that fight: if I had been, I would have knocked him out in six rounds. "Today I sent him to the hospital," I said after the fight. "Next time I'll put him in the morgue." I can't apologize for what happened: this is what we do—we're boxers and these are the risks we take when we get in the ring. I knew that and Lampkin knew that, too.

Only later did I find out he'd ended up in intensive care, where they'd given him all sorts of neurological and clinical tests. General Torrijos had even called to congratulate him for fighting well. I went to see him in the hospital, and one of the nurses said, "Oh, Señor Durán, Mr. Lampkin was in very bad shape. We had to save his life." He couldn't talk, couldn't remember anything. When he finally woke up, though, he asked for coffee, and the only brand they had was one sold in Panama called Café Durán.

"No, I don't want Durán coffee!" he told the nurses. "Please, no!"

His manager wanted a rematch as quickly as possible. Why? I have no idea, when even his own trainer was saying it would be four to six months before he'd be able to fight again. He went home to Portland in a wheelchair, his eyes still puffy from the beating. He needed to go to therapy every day and walk using those bars they have for rehabilitation. He had swelling at the back of his brain and his manager was talking about a rematch! His trainer was right: it was going to take a long time. He didn't fight for another seven months, and he was never the same again after our fight. We never did have that rematch.

For me, it was my forty-second knockout in fifty professional fights. I made $75,000 tax-free, plus training expenses. But I'd also reached the point where I could not make that weight anymore, which meant a conversation with Eleta. I was twenty-five now and my body was different—at least that's what I told him. My natural weight was 152 pounds, which would make life difficult in the lightweight division, where the limit was 135. Even when I was training hard I could barely make 140, the super-lightweight maximum. The truth was, the other reason I started to fight in higher weight classifications was that I needed the money to take care of my family and the heavier divisions paid more. Thank God everything worked out in the end, but first I had some business to take care of at lower weights.

Two fights later, I traveled to Managua, Nicaragua, for a fight on August 2, 1975, against Pedro Mendoza—there they called him "El Toro," The Bull. It was a non-title fight, light welterweights. A few days before the fight, a policeman showed up at the hotel and told me General Anastasio Somoza, the president, wanted to meet me. Somoza's palace was nearby, and when I arrived, the general, who was a big guy—much bigger than me—didn't even look at me. Then he said: "Durán, don't kill El Toro."

"If I don't kill him," I said, "he's going to kill me. If I don't knock him out, he's going to knock me out." The general didn't have much of an answer to that. I wasn't going to back down for anyone—I didn't care how important they were. My wife just laughed when I told her—"You're crazy, Durán!"

I came into the ring in a colorful robe and the Nicaraguans started taunting me, calling me a butterfly. *La mariposa! La mariposa!* Butterfly, my ass. I knocked the guy out two minutes into the first round. Immediately this drunk woman climbs into the ring and starts berating me—"I hate you! I hate you! You're the worst person to visit Nicaragua!"— before falling on her face. The crowd thought I'd done it, went berserk, and tried to lynch me. I was lucky the police grabbed hold of me and escorted me to the dressing room before anyone could get near me. I got out of there as fast as I could and flew back to Panama the next morning, relieved to be out of that crazy place. I would never fight there again—never been back. Later I heard that the woman was Eleanora Baca, El Toro's fiancée. All I know is, she was trying to hurt me—I didn't want any trouble.

I returned to New York for the first time in almost three years when I defeated Edwin Viruet by ten-round decision on September 30, 1975. It's a date inscribed in the memory of every boxing fan, because we were on the undercard at the Nassau Coliseum in Uniondale, New York, to the main event being shown on closed-circuit television: the "Thrilla in Manila" between Joe Frazier and Muhammad Ali. I stuck around to watch, and I'll never forget it.

That same year, I would first cross paths with another legend in boxing, Don King, when Eleta signed a three-fight package with him to promote my fights, starting with my lightweight title defense against Leoncio Ortíz in Puerto Rico in December. I won by knockout in the fifteenth round, but I would have done so earlier if he hadn't run away from me so much. My corner told me to take it easy on him in the thirteenth, so I could build my strength to knock him out in the fourteenth or fifteenth, and that's exactly what I did. A right cross to the chin and he was finished. I was pleased, because after my last two fights in Puerto Rico had been won on a decision, I wanted to prove to the fans there that I still lived up to the name Manos de Piedra. I didn't want to be remembered as one of those fighters who just went looking for the points. Every time I went into the ring, I wanted to knock the guy out cold, and it was important for me to get back to doing that again.

Then that idiot Viruet got in my face as I was going back to the dressing room, challenging me for another shot at the title. Why? I'd already beaten him. I got annoyed and took a few swings at him for good measure, and it took the police to break things up. Sure, I said, I would love to give him another chance. So I could punish him some more! And that's exactly what would happen.

Viruet was a nobody. Ali, on the other hand, was somebody. Like everyone else, I'd been watching him for years. I finally met him the following year when I was training in Miami Beach to fight Saoul Mamby in May 1976. Ali was there to film the movie *The Greatest*. One day, a guard stops me at the door of the 5th St. Gym and tells me to wait, they were busy filming. After ten minutes, they let me through— I was lucky because I was the only boxer they let in to train. While I was minding my own business, Ali kept watching me. I hit the speed bag and the heavy bag for a while and then I started skipping rope.

"I've never seen a man jump rope like that," he said. "Quite extraordinary."

Afterward, a few female police officers showed up and he started talking to them playfully and giving them kisses. Ali's wife was there, and I overheard her say, "You did it and now I'm going to leave you." Even with my sketchy English I understood what she was saying, and I'll never forget it. "You and me are through." I just stared at them, thinking, You can't say that—he's the greatest of all time!

In the years to come, after I became more famous, Ali couldn't fill up Madison Square Garden like he used to, so they put my name on the undercard to draw fans and hope they would stick around to watch Ali. By then he knew, and I knew, that people had come to see Roberto Durán, not Muhammad Ali. But this was still in the future.

Miami Beach had become one of my favorite places outside Panama. I loved New York, of course, but Miami was special ever since my first fight there in 1975, when I knocked out José Peterson. The food was similar to food back home, and so were the customs—and the language, of course—and the Cuban people who lived there were great to me. My first friend there was this black Cuban guy I met about a month or two before defending my WBA lightweight title against Vilomar Fernandez at the Fontainebleau Hotel in January 1977. I'd go whoring around Miami with him, and there was a strip club he'd take me to.

Although I was playing around more and enjoying my time in Miami on my own, it did nothing to affect my performance in the ring, and I took Fernandez out in the thirteenth round. Knockout—*boom!*—retained my title. Two more victories, and here came Viruet, back for more. Apparently he hadn't had enough punishment. I'd beaten the crap out of him once already and now he was saying he'd beaten me when we fought two years before and he made me miss and look bad. He said he was going to put me into retirement, but I guess he hadn't read enough of my history. *I'm* the boxer who forced fighters to retire. And he would pay for what he'd said. I came in fit, at 134½ pounds. I hit him with a lot of body shots to start the fight, through the first four rounds. I kept the pressure on him throughout the fight, but he did a good job of moving in and out to avoid getting hurt. I had him on the ropes a lot, and although he went the distance, I was always in control. My victory over him in 1977 was the eleventh defense of my WBA lightweight title.

But I had bigger plans, and bigger men to face, including de Jesús for the third time. Don King—Eleta was talking to him regularly now—had floated the idea of New York, at Madison Square Garden, or Miami, but he settled on Las Vegas. Wherever it was to be, I wanted that son of a bitch badly. It was another grudge match, and this time I was hoping he wouldn't run like he did in the first rematch.

For months before the fight he talked shit about me. De Jesús had won the World Boxing Council belt after beating Ishimatsu Suzuki, and had three more defenses, and he thought that gave him permission to say what he wanted about anyone. I just wanted to shut his big mouth.

It was the first time in the history of Las Vegas there had been two Latin fighters on the marquee at Caesars Palace. We were fighting for the big prize: the undisputed world lightweight title. Nobody had unified the division since 1971. For me, this was a real chance to make history, not to mention a real chance for de Jesús to get his ass kicked again.

De Jesús was having the same problem as me in making

the weight, but it was worse for him since he was too muscular. When you have big arms and a big chest, it's especially hard to make weight. Because we were both training in Miami, I could see he was struggling—you just had to look at his physique. I drew great strength from this. Whenever the training was getting tough, I knew it was nothing compared with what de Jesús was going through. "This guy," I told Plomo, "is not going to beat me."

Maybe de Jesús knew that, too. I heard he had to really work hard until the last minute to make weight. I had to shed fifteen pounds in a month, which wasn't such a big deal for me since I was used to it, and came in at 134¼. He was 134, with that big mouth and all. But I knew he was in trouble and so did he, which is why he tried to start some shit before we even got in the ring. On the day of the weigh-in, there was almost a big fight between my guys and his. He threw a punch at me with his bare fists, I swung back, somebody waved a chair in the air—it was all about to kick off.

Maybe Esteban was trying to psyche me out, but it was all *mierda*, bullshit. He hired *brujos*, witch doctors, to cast a Santería hex on me, but I told them where to go. I think they were even scattering some kind of Santería dust in the ring as I was warming up. It just made me laugh.

There were almost 5,000 fans at Caesars Palace that night, lots from Panama cheering me on, and just as many from Puerto Rico rooting for de Jesús. Don King said people from both countries were showing up with suitcases full of money to bet on their favorite fighter.

The advantage I had is that when he'd knocked me down a second time in Panama, he'd caught me off guard. I'd just wanted to knock him out and hadn't taken the time to study him properly. Instead, I'd just traded punches. The third time around I wasn't going to do that even though that's what he expected. They had everything planned, thinking he was going to knock me out with all that witchcraft nonsense. So I just boxed him, always waiting for an opening. I knew that's what I had to do—he wasn't very intelligent when you boxed him. It was to his advantage to get into a brawl. I wasn't going to do that.

I hit him with a jab with my first punch and he smiled. He wasn't going to be smiling for much of the night. Ninety seconds into the fight, he was bleeding from the nose. I almost knocked him out with a left hook at the end of the round. As the fight went on I could have knocked him out sooner, but I needed to be cautious since I hadn't fought in four months. I would have fought him all night if I'd had to. I knew I was going to win.

By the seventh round I knew he was tired. I was, too, but I was holding some strength in reserve. And the fight went exactly as I'd planned. In the tenth he went down again, this time with a body shot to the ribs. His feet lifted off the ground. I could feel my fist grind into his body—can you imagine what it must have felt like for him? De Jesús had nothing. He was reaching, pulling punches. In the eleventh I kept pounding him with body blows. That kills a boxer: it sucks the air out of you, sucks the life out of you, and de Jesús did not have much life left in this fight. He wasn't going to last fifteen rounds.

Then the twelfth. When he went to throw a left hook, I hit him with a right cross counterpunch to the jaw that dropped him. He crawled back to a neutral corner, got up in plenty of time, but he was done. And then I went after him like a hurricane. I hit him eleven, twelve times, didn't miss once. I knew I had him. I knew he was going to go. I knew I had to kill him as soon as possible. It would only be a matter of time. He went down again. De Jesús co-trainer finally threw in the towel and ran into the ring to stop him from taking more punishment while I had him against the ropes. The referee didn't stop it, de Jesús' people did. I wasn't surprised when he went down. That's why they call me Manos de Piedra. Hands of Stone.

I almost knocked somebody else out that night, too. After the fight, one of de Jesús' *manzanillos* jumped into the ring and tried to start something. I thought about punching him but backed off. Maybe it was one of those *brujos*. Santería, my ass. At 2:32 of that twelfth round, I joined the heavyweight Muhammad Ali and middleweight Rodrigo Váldez as the only undisputed champions in boxing.

The January 30, 1978, issue of *Sports Illustrated* reported:

> Moving fluidly and jabbing, slipping punches and countering rather than swarming over De Jesús, he stalked him, relentlessly wearing him down and coolly destroying him with short, savage punches

to the body. For 11 rounds Durán bested the classic boxer at his own game, robbing him of his speed and his will to fight, and only then did he permit himself the luxury of putting De Jesús away.

That night I was all by myself on the big stage. I could never erase the loss, but that night I erased de Jesús, and that felt pretty good.

I'd won my thirty-first consecutive fight. My sixty-first victory in sixty-two fights, my eleventh knockout in twelve title defenses. But most important, I had my revenge against the only man to beat me. And I had a lot of money, again: $100,000 after taxes, plus Don King's $1,000 bonus under the table. I wasn't so bothered about a Puerto Rico–Panama rivalry. He was their idol, but I wasn't as popular as I had been in Panama after the crap people still talked about me after losing the first fight. My interest was in winning and then going drinking somewhere. And shutting up all the Panamanians who were talking bad about me. And that's exactly what I did.

Of course I celebrated! Roberto Durán always celebrates! A few hours after the fight I was walking around Caesars Palace with no shirt, barefoot, a towel around my neck and a bottle of champagne in my hand. Two old people looked at me in the elevator and didn't seem to like what they saw. I didn't care. *Dios mío!* I thought New York was a big city with a lot of lights. But this place was crazy, with so many beautiful women. I hopped in the car with some of my buddies and went off to party and get drunk—like the Americans say, Vegas never closes. I even ran into de Jesús and invited him back to my room to play dominoes—he said he couldn't beat me in the ring but he could take me at dominoes. But he never showed up. Later I got dressed up in a tuxedo and a ruffled shirt to catch Sammy Davis, Jr.'s nightclub act, drank some more, and at three in the morning had a large steak. What did I care? I wasn't going to train tomorrow, or the next day. I was now the best pound-per-pound fighter in the world. I had had three great fights with de Jesús, the first man to beat me, but I didn't bear him a grudge. The world would see that a few years later.

After this, I had another fight in New York. It was Viruet, not Edwin, but his brother Adolfo. I guess they wanted me to beat up the entire family. Sure, why not? It was hard, as usual, to make weight, but it was harder for me to fight at all because now all of my opponents were running away. Nobody wanted to fight me. They were making me become a salsa singer.

It was a non-title fight, so I was able to weigh in at 142, seven pounds heavier than the lightweight limit. I felt good, and not just because I wasn't forced to beat the scale. I'd be fighting at Madison Square Garden again for the first time in six years. And I was getting a nice payday: $100,000 after taxes.

Viruet came to fight that night, but he wasn't going to beat me. I caught him with some good shots in the eighth to end the round, and I knew he was in trouble. I certainly wasn't, even though I'd had a point taken away in the seventh because the referee said I hit Viruet below the belt. After the tenth and final round, both judges and referee Arthur Mercante had me winning with a unanimous decision.

I hated both those Viruet brothers, and they didn't like me. Edwin came after me because I said some shit about his father after the fight, but the security people were able to break it up. He was lucky. Maybe I could have beaten both brothers in one night—that would have been another one for the record books!

I was more than ready to move up to welterweight by the time I fought Monroe Brooks on December 8, 1978. In fact, I weighed 147 for that fight, twelve pounds more than the lightweight limit. It didn't matter, though, and I ripped him up pretty good, with a number of head shots that connected over seven rounds, before I finished him off with a body punch in the eighth. A left hook to the body just below the rib cage and he was done.

And I was done as a lightweight, too. I had a reputation for enjoying the party scene, which I didn't mind at all, but it did mean that Freddie Brown had to get to work on me before every fight. He had already forced me to take off more than twenty-five pounds six or seven times. He trained me like I was in the army. "I no strong! I no strong!" I would tell him. He wanted to starve me; I wanted to eat. The problem was, I got bored with the lack of real competition. Sometimes I wondered whether we would ever actually get into the ring! So what happened? I got fat, and then it would be hard to make weight. I loved to eat, I liked to drink beer, and I loved Coca-Cola. When I trained for a fight, I would sit with Fula and the rest of my family and I wouldn't be able to eat what they ate. I'd look at them and say, "Eat that sandwich— it's good. Enjoy it"—and then they'd feel bad because I couldn't eat.

But they were right to feel bad. I was suffering. Sometimes I wouldn't eat for days. I'd stick lemons in my mouth, hoping to burn away the fat. Of course it would have been easier just to stick to a disciplined diet, but I couldn't help myself. When my brother Pototo was staying at the hotel, I used to ask him to buy me six-packs of Coke and I'd hide the cans under my bed. Sometimes there'd be thirty or forty Coke cans under there! Or I'd hide them in my luggage so Freddie Brown wouldn't see them. After the weigh-in, I'd take them out and start drinking Coca-Cola until I couldn't swallow any more.

Freddie Brown drove me crazy. He wouldn't let me eat anything, and I still had to keep training, sparring. I had no strength—I was dying from hunger. My brother, bless him. I'd often say, "*Hermanito*"—little brother—"when you go down to eat, could you bring me back a bread roll or two?" And he'd grab a couple and put them in his pocket so Freddie wouldn't see, and I'd wash them down with a glass of water. No butter. That would ease the hunger pangs so I could get to sleep. And after the weigh-in, we'd want a treat: ice cream and Coca-Cola, all mixed up, and both of us would dig in.

But Brown was so paranoid, he kept a scale in my room,

the same one I'd used since turning pro, called *la romana*—it would come back into my life after I retired. Brown wanted to make sure I wasn't gaining weight when he wasn't looking, so when I finished running, he'd weigh me. When I had breakfast, he'd weigh me. Before I sparred, he'd weigh me. After I sparred, he'd weigh me. He'd even try to train me in the soldiers' barracks in Panama, where he thought he could control things. *Chuleta!* That's what he thought! I'd get my friends to sneak steaks in! It was such a pain in the ass to make weight. Besides, I was getting bored with the division: I'd successfully defended my title twelve times and I no longer felt challenged. I knew there were bigger guys out there, and that meant more money. Eleta was talking about the possibility of my taking on the WBA welterweight champ José "Pipino" Cuevas later in the year, but a better fight would come my way.

So much for my lightweight title. I wanted other opportunities, and I could no longer make weight even if I tried. I gave up my undisputed lightweight championship in February 1979. And now, two months later, I was fighting an American named Jimmy Heair in Las Vegas, in my first fight in seven years without the title of world champion. It was a ten-round preliminary bout, and I won in a unanimous decision. Of course, Vegas was a big boxing city, and during that trip I visited the great American boxer Joe Louis, who was in poor health by then and in a wheelchair.

Back in Panama, I picked up an unusual pet: a lion. I love animals and I like having them around—dogs, especially

English bulldogs, birds, iguanas . . . But this pet was going to be very different. I had a Mexican friend who owned a circus in Panama. I loved visiting it and messing around with the lions. But eventually business started to go bad and my friend had to sell two lions to a zoo in Panama. He gave me an eagle, but a lion was what I really wanted. Then I heard one of the female lions was pregnant. I took the eagle to Roberto, the guy who ran the zoo, and offered him the eagle for the lion. I came home with a lion cub, and we named him Walla. He would drink two or three quarts of milk a day. I had his claws filed down and his mane cut, and I had to have him neutered. We managed to domesticate him, and I used to take him everywhere. I really loved taking him to carnivals and having people come up to look at him. I even bought a big truck so I could take him places. One day I took him back to see Roberto.

He looked scared. "How did you do this?"

"I domesticated him," I said.

His mouth was open. I picked up the lion. "Now I want to see what I gave you."

The eagle spread his wings. They were huge. "I'm going to have to let him go," said Roberto. "He's just too big."

But Walla was great, living at home where everyone played with him, including the kids and my eighty-year-old neighbor. Once a week or so, I'd give him a bath—we raised him like a pet dog. When Chavo was about seventeen months old, he toddled out onto the patio, and my wife yelled, "Be

careful—the lion's loose!" Next thing we see, Walla is licking
Chavo, affectionately giving him a tongue bath.

That lion was so smart. He was able to open the door to
the house with his paws. He got along so well with our bull-
dog, Jango, they slept together, ate together. In retrospect, it
was incredible—you'd never be allowed to do that now, not
even in Panama! But we were never scared. Even my wife
would put milk in her cupped hands and let him drink. His
tongue was like sandpaper! I was the only man in Panama,
Eleta would joke, who could clear the streets by taking a lion
out for a walk. But I was the king of Panama, so why not have
a lion in my entourage?

I did take him to the InterContinental Hotel in Panama
once. I left him there for the day while I went out, and when
the maid came in to clean the room, she screamed like crazy.
When I got back, I apologized to her—I didn't know she was
going to clean the room. I think it was probably the most
memorable day of her life.

Walla was getting bigger by the day and so was I. I left
him behind to go to New York again, this time to train to
fight Carlos Palomino. I'd gone up to 147 and fought against
four easy opponents, waiting for a shot at the welterweight
title, when the opportunity came up to fight Palomino in
Madison Square Garden in June 1979. He was a former WBC
welterweight champion, who had won the title from John H.
Stracey of Britain and defended it several times. Although he
wasn't still the champion, he was the number-one contender.

Freddie Brown had now been in my corner for five years, and he knew, as I did, that this was a big one for me. It was in a place I loved, obviously, but it was also my chance to prove that I could still carry power at a heavier weight. Before losing his title to Wilfred Benítez, who beat him by split decision for the WBC welterweight title in January 1979, Palomino had said he would retire by the time he was thirty to pursue a career in acting. When he fought me, he was only two months shy of his thirtieth birthday, and I made it my goal to help him fulfill his wish.

One of the reasons I love New York is that you can bump into anyone at any time, not like in Panama, where we all live very separate lives, depending on which social class we're in. One day, our camp decided to go play softball in Central Park. This guy's walking toward us—it's Robert De Niro. I couldn't believe my eyes. Franco, one of the guys in my camp, says to him, "This is my friend, the boxer Stone Hands."

"Pleasure to meet you," says De Niro. And then he says, "Can I play softball with you guys? Can I bring some of my friends? Give me an hour." Half an hour later, we see a bunch of people with him—they're all actors in town with him to film *Raging Bull*. My mouth is wide open.

"Let's kick their asses," says one of my friends.

De Niro replies, "Wanna bet? What about loser pays for dinner?"

I knew if we lost, I could bring him to Victor's. It would be great publicity, and I wouldn't have to pick up the tab.

But we ended up kicking their asses. So I call Victor to

save us a table for twenty, and once there, De Niro says, "Champagne for everyone!" We drank it like it was water. By the time we were done eating and drinking, the tab was over $7,000. It was a good thing we didn't have to pick up the check.

De Niro invited me back to his apartment, a penthouse in the Mayflower. People like Joe Pesci were there; he was also in *Raging Bull*. Finally, I had to tell De Niro I couldn't drink anymore—I had to be up at five a.m. to run.

I loved watching movies. Back then, there weren't a lot of movies in Spanish, but in New York there was a Blockbuster off Broadway where I'd go buy twenty or thirty VHS movies at a time. Each time, I came back to Panama with a suitcase full, mostly action movies, and the family used to fight over which one to watch first.

I got a bit part in a movie myself. For a change of scenery, I was training briefly in Los Angeles. Sly Stallone started hanging around the gym—he was a big boxing fan, and liked me a lot, and they offered me a part in *Rocky II* sparring against him.

When filming got under way, Stallone and I spent a lot of time practicing, and I used to work him over in the sparring sessions. He tried to skip like I did, but he couldn't even though he tried hard—he was a big guy. He was in good shape and taking the filming seriously, and I think he started believing he could keep up with me in the ring. *Chuleta*, right! He wasn't going to hurt me. During one of the sparring sessions, I tagged him pretty good and I think he got the message. "Durán, don't hit me in the nose," he told me. "Remember, I'm an actor, not a boxer." He even wore headgear, just in case—I didn't. In the film you can hear Rocky's trainer yelling, "Speed, speed! Catch that punk!" and "Can't you catch that little squirt? Cut off the ring! Get the lead out." That was fiction, just a lot of fake boxing, but the reality was that Stallone said sparring with me felt like his head was being lowered into a Cuisinart blender.

I met a lot of Hollywood people in Palm Springs—Kirk Douglas, Bob Hope, Trini Lopez—because that's where Don King would send me to train. I used to love being around them, imagining what the guys back home would think—Durán, the kid who stole mangoes for a living, hanging out with Hollywood royalty. To show off for them, I would hit the speed bag with my head. They say the hands are quicker than the eyes, so I would work on making my eyes just as quick. I wouldn't lose sight of the bag. The gyms would fill up, especially because people loved the way I jumped rope. I would drop down into a squat position and then shoot back up. Then I would cross my hands over while I skipped. It took tremendous strength, speed, and coordination. I came up with that technique all on my own.

But my focus at that time was on Palomino and making a mark in a new division. It was on the undercard of a nationally televised world heavyweight title fight between Larry Holmes and Mike Weaver, but everybody was talking about me and Palomino. Muhammad Ali had retired the year before, and boxing fans were now showing more interest in the lower weight classes. And I was a star, of course. But there were a lot of people who thought I might not be able to handle a fighter of Palomino's ability because of the move up in weight. I paid no attention. I guess Palomino was expecting me to disrespect him at the press conference, but I went easy on him. I even asked him for an autograph for my son. "I feared the worst," Palomino told reporters. "I figured he'd start his usual name-calling act. But he walks up to me, shakes my hand, and tells me that he respects me as a fighter. He caught me off guard and . . . that took the fire out of me."

It was more than words that took the fire out of him. It was my fists, even though his reach was two and a half inches longer. I knocked him right into retirement. It was a great night from the start. The crowd was behind me and gave me a great ovation as I entered the ring. I was aggressive early, and it was clear it was going to be a good night for me. I pounded him inside, hurt him. I had too much speed for him and he couldn't handle my feints. By the third round, I was laughing. By the fifth round, I could hear the crowd chant, *"Doo-ran! Doo-ran!"* as they waited to see Palomino go down.

I gave them what they wanted seconds into the sixth round when I dropped him with an overhand right. It happened so fast that Ray Arcel was still at the top of the ring apron. It was only the second time Palomino had been down in thirty-three fights. He got up quickly, but only to take more punishment. He was bleeding behind the left ear. I almost dropped him with another right at the end of the round. By the tenth and final round, I was laughing and taunting him. He had nothing for El Cholo. I won every round; maybe I won every minute. Two judges had me winning 99–90 and the third 99–91. I knew then that this was where I belonged.

At the end of the fight I fell to my knees to give thanks. Then I got up and hugged Palomino. I stood up on the ring apron, grabbed a small Panamanian flag, and acknowledged all the fans who'd been cheering for me.

"Durán [brought] a sense of almost surrealistic beauty to savagery, fighting for the first time as a welterweight," Pat Putnam wrote in *Sports Illustrated*,

> and, after ten brutal rounds, chasing Carlos Palomino, the former WBC champion, into retirement. . . . [Durán] bewildered Palomino with flicking head and shoulder feints; he battered him with punches thrown at blinding speed. At times, just for fun, he feinted from the left, feinted from the right, and then, with Palomino in a flux of frantic confusion, stepped back and flashed a wolfish grin as Palomino untangled himself.

There was one thing Palomino got right that night. After he admitted to Larry Merchant of HBO that he wasn't what he used to be, Merchant asked him if he thought I was going to be the next welterweight champion of the world.

"I believe so," he said.

"He doesn't speak English very well," Merchant said of me that night, "but he speaks boxing as well as any man who's ever lived."

I was now 66–1 and ready for more.

But the celebration after the fight took a sad turn that night. While I'd been in training, Chaflán, my friend and mentor from my childhood days, died. They kept the news from me until after the fight because they didn't want me to be upset. Fula finally broke the news. I was sad, even cried a little bit. Back in Panama, I went to see his elderly mother and his twin brother and gave them some money. Chaflán was a good man who did a lot for me. He taught me about adversity. He always said I had a friend in him. He always promised, with a smile on his face, that *"todo estará bien."* Everything will be okay.

FOUR

SUGAR RAY
MEETS
CHARLES
MANSON

In early 1980, I got a call from Eleta. "Do you know about this boxer who's a sensation among the gringos? He's a proper star, and a terrific boxer. Do you want to fight him for a world title?"

"Of course."

"He's very fast . . ."

"So he's fast. Blah, blah."

"No, I mean *fast*. He's a quick black kid."

"I don't care. What's his name?"

"Sugar Ray Leonard."

In those days, that was how fights got arranged—one call and it was fixed up. To tell the truth, I'd never heard of the guy. I wasn't sitting at home, checking out every boxer on the planet. I didn't waste my time thinking about who might be out there—my job was to train for the next fight and win it. Everything else I left up to Eleta. All I knew was, I was destroying everyone they put in front of me; some fast little black kid from the United States wasn't going to beat me.

Before I knew what had happened, the media had broken the story that I was going to fight Leonard, and it all kicked off big-time. I was at home in Panama watching the news with Flaco Bala, and all they could talk about was this American kid, Sugar Ray Leonard, and all the money he was going to make fighting me. I was immediately pissed off. Why was he getting all the money? And why all the attention? Didn't they know about me, Manos de Piedra? Flaco Bala said he saw a look in my eyes, a mean look he'd never seen before.

"I hate him," I told Flaco Bala, even though I'd barely heard of the guy. "I will beat the living shit out of him."

"Don't hate him," Flaco Bala said. "It's just the way things are in America. We'll beat him, and beating him, we'll beat the system."

I said nothing, but inside I still felt the same. Leonard was a pretty boy, undefeated (27–0), and everyone liked him for his charm and showmanship, like Muhammad Ali. He had all these endorsements from American companies like 7UP, and the media loved him for his good looks. I obviously didn't have the same things going for me because I didn't speak English, and I wasn't going to learn just for some shitty commercial.

Ray was the Big American Hero, a Superman, a god. And here was this Latino nobody could figure out, except that he was a genuine force of nature. But they could not ignore me in the ring: 71–1, with fifty-six knockouts, a legend already. Combined, our records were 98–1, and I'd done most of the work. I didn't give a crap about the American Hero. Or

Superman. All I wanted to do was defeat the pinup boy of the United States. As Don King, my promoter, put it, I was "the little killer." I had three months to prepare for the fight, and I promised myself I would train harder than I had ever done before. I was going to show them that if you underestimate Durán, you are making a big mistake.

At this time, Latino fighters were only starting to get attention in the United States. There were popular Puerto Rican fighters like de Jesús on the East Coast, but a lot of people in New York resented Puerto Ricans, who were seen as economic migrants in search of a better life. Most Americans still weren't aware of what was happening with the Mexican and other Hispanic fighters in Texas and California and on the West Coast—fighters like me, José Nápoles, and other international stars. But my record meant that people were paying attention to me above all others, and my saying just how I was going to beat the crap out of Leonard only made them come back for more. Muhammad Ali was coming to the end of his career and no one was interested in seeing an old fighter in the ring—they all wanted to see Durán. But all the American journalists could write about was Leonard this, Leonard that . . . They were still infatuated with the 1976 Montreal Olympics, where five members of the U.S. boxing team—Leonard, Howard Davis, Jr., Leo Randolph, the Spinks brothers—had won gold medals. If there was any interest in foreign fighters, it was in the guys making money in Europe, like Carlos Monzón.

Leonard didn't know much about me, either, since I was

a lightweight and he was a welterweight—we'd never even fought on the same card. Later he'd say he first saw me fight in Las Vegas, when he'd been sitting near Jackie Gleason. Leonard was a big fan of Gleason—loved him in *The Honeymooners*—and he'd turned to Gleason and said, "Hey, I'm going to fight him." And Gleason had said, "Don't you ever say that again. Don't fight that guy—he's a monster! He'll kill you." Leonard was so offended by this, he even quit watching *The Honeymooners*. But Gleason was right. Leonard had plenty to worry about.

I wasn't short of motivation to beat him: for a start, there was the money. I was getting only $1.5 million, whereas Leonard was getting more than $8 million, but the closer we got to the fight, the less I cared about that and the more I cared about the opportunity to write my name in history. When I beat Leonard, as I knew I would, I would have done something no other boxer in history had achieved: beaten the undefeated American golden boy. I started telling reporters that I would fight for nothing, that I had no respect for Leonard, that he had a big mouth and talked too much—maybe if I punched him in the face enough times, he would shut up. The press liked that: now they could see Leonard had a real fight ahead of him.

In a lot of ways, I was Mike Tyson before Mike Tyson came along. Fighters would take one look at me and crap in their pants. Leonard would be no different. It was starting to dawn on the Americans that they'd never come across anything like me before—this eerie, deadly being with his jet-black hair and his dark eyes and his bad intentions. "El Diablo," they called me: the Devil. I wasn't going to do anything to make them think otherwise.

So when I faced Leonard, I was the "other": the outsider, the mysterious foreigner, fighting the Great American Hero who was just so dignified and upstanding and such a wonderful personality and so media-friendly and all that crap. Good versus evil, and I was the bad guy. It was like all those movies I used to watch when I was a *pelao* in Panama: cowboys versus Indians. *Chuleta*, I had Mexican blood in me—close enough. The best part was, I could not give a damn. They could write what they liked about me—I couldn't read English.

I never got involved in the financial side of my career, but whatever they were saying about me, good or bad, it seemed to be generating a lot of interest. The fight had even brought two rival promoters together for the first time, Don King and Bob Arum, who handled Leonard and had set up fights for Muhammad Ali and other famous boxers. King and Arum didn't like each other, but they did like money. And this fight was going to make a lot of money for a lot of people.

Before the 1980s, all the big fights were on prime-time TV, but now promoters were asking fight fans to pay money for the best fights. The pay-per-view and closed-circuit TV markets were just starting up, although, until then, mostly for Ali's big fights, especially those against Joe Frazier. But now Durán versus Leonard was getting its share of attention. Arum said this fight would be the beginning of a revolution in boxing and television, and he was right. It was going to be seen on closed-circuit TV in more than 250 theaters and arenas, and also on two pay-per-view channels in Los Angeles and Columbus, Ohio. ABC Sports wouldn't show it live but would air it later, on July 19, on *Wide World of Sports*.

In the meantime, there was plenty of time to hype the fight, and it obviously helped sales if there was bad blood between us. Things started out okay, but it all changed in April when we went to the Waldorf Astoria in New York for King, Eleta, and the others to set the date for June 20, 1980, at the Olympic Stadium in Montreal: "The Brawl in Montreal," they'd dubbed it. With the cameras flashing, Leonard smiled at me and said, "Hi." This was the first time I'd met him, but already I hated him.

I sat down in front of the microphones. "I came here to fight," I told the reporters. "I didn't come here to clown around. Tell Leonard when he fights me, he's going to have a real fight on his hands."

I think I got Leonard scared right from the start, and I did everything I could to mess with his head. We had on these oversize gloves with the sponsor's logo on them, the kind used for publicity shots, and even though we were just meant to stand there, posing with them, I kept hitting him in the head, each time a bit harder. I don't think he'd been expecting that. They had food for us at the press conference. I pulled fruit to bits with my bare hands, stabbed my fork in my steak, and fell on it. It was all part of the plan—to make him think I was crazy. What was I going to do next? I knew he could box, so if I was going to win, I'd have to get inside his head and break him down mentally. We were going to fight on my terms and that meant a street fight.

And then he started to talk shit. "I'm not just going to beat Roberto Durán. I'm going to kill him." When the reporters asked him about my dark eyes, he tried to make a joke of it: Eyes couldn't hurt you, he said—only fists. He said he was too fast for me, that he was king of the division.

Chuleta, que payaso. What a clown. I called him a *maricón*, faggot. I had never fought a man I liked, and now I hated Leonard, too. He was stupid to say all that shit. I didn't care about his undefeated record. All he had fought before me were dead people. Now he was going to fight Roberto Durán, and he was very much alive.

To begin with, I trained in New York at Gleason's Gym, before moving to Grossinger's in the Catskills. I didn't know the place well then, but it had a great reputation with American boxers. I was the seventh world champion to train there. It was such a big resort—it had everything: facilities for handball, tennis, skiing, ice skating, and other sports as well.

And it was very quiet there, which was perfect. The only people I came across were groups of elderly Jewish people on vacation and I didn't see them much. I went to the restaurant twice a day and there weren't many people in it, which was just as well, because Freddie Brown was being very strict about my diet. All he allowed me was steak and steamed vegetables. And water—gallons and gallons of water. Just to break up the routine, I tried the Jewish chicken soup now and then. I liked it, but what I really craved was some good home cooking.

Brown was working me harder than ever before. His idea was that training camp should feel just like jail. At least in the Catskills the mountain air was cool and refreshing, and I had Kevin Rooney, who would later train Mike Tyson, as one of my sparring partners, and he was a good guy. My salsa buddy Rubén Blades came up to hang out with us, too. We played dominoes, and sometimes he would translate for me when the gringo journalists came to cover the training sessions.

I didn't like speaking English—it was too easy to say something that could be misunderstood. But sometimes when I spoke Spanish they understood. "I fight for *la plata*," I told them one day. Money. But of course this fight was different because I wanted the money *and* the title.

I kept a large bongo drum at the foot of my bed and at night, after training, I played the timbales to remind me of home and to keep my spirits up. To help take my mind off the fight in the evening, I'd play salsa records, which would make me think about my mother, Clara, back home in Panama, and how much I loved her and wanted to take care of her. I'd bought her a house; now I wanted more—for her, for me, for my family. And then I'd fall asleep until Freddie Brown would come and wake me up to go running in the dark. And then we'd start all over again. I talked a lot to Flaco Bala and some of the others in my camp: I knew what tricks Leonard was going to try and I was going to be ready for them.

In the past, I'd screwed around a lot before fights, spent a lot of money on drinking and women. Not this time. I realized how important this fight was, and I wasn't going to let anything distract me. This was my chance to make the world take notice, and I wasn't going to blow it. I was in the best shape I'd ever been since becoming too big to fight as a lightweight.

We traveled to Montreal three weeks before the fight. I worked very hard—came close to knocking out one of my sparring partners. But I made one big mistake. A boxer depends on his legs: they need to be strong, so I started to train in cowboy boots to make them stronger—it made running up and down hills much harder. But it also messed up my back. I was taken to a hospital in New York and made to lie down underneath a contraption that looked like a laser—it was like that scene in the Bond movie *Goldfinger*! But at least it got rid of the pain.

I thought I was playing some good mind games on Leonard, but you wouldn't believe all the tricks they tried to make sure he won—even putting the fight on in Montreal, where he'd won his Olympic gold medal and everyone loved him. But when I showed up wearing a T-shirt that read "Bonjour Montreal!" and then signed autographs, I won everyone over. I did all my workouts in public—we set up at a downtown shopping center, and thousands of fans came and watched me train. They loved to see how I jumped rope and hit the speed bag so fast. Even though I couldn't speak English, I managed to talk to people, and we got along just fine. I was surprised they weren't more stuck on the American, but in fact, it was the tough guy they warmed to. They loved everything I stood for. The bottom line: They loved a badass.

In Montreal, like in the Catskills, we had a great camp. Even though we were staying in a hotel, Fula took care of my diet, doing all the shopping and cooking for me. She was five months pregnant with our second son, Robin, so we didn't go out much, just stayed in our room, relaxing. And when I trained, I concentrated on winding Leonard up. How? I knew he was sending his brother to spy on me—I could see him taking notes—so I pushed all Leonard's buttons. I knew I could turn the fight into a brawl.

I even went after his wife. One day, I bumped into Leonard and her walking down the street with Angelo Dundee, his trainer, and his wife. I gave Leonard's wife the middle finger. I told Leonard I was going to cut his balls off. I knew I'd gotten to him. He wanted to fight me on the street, there and then. It was all meant to drive Leonard crazy, and it worked. Later I found out that that was when he really started to worry. I was a lot more intelligent than people were giving me credit for, and I knew if Leonard tried to fight me instead of boxing, he'd be in trouble. Angelo Dundee would call it one of the best con jobs in boxing.

Leonard didn't know how to handle all this shit. He'd always been the pretty boy, the guy smiling in front of the camera, the good guy—the guy who was on top, in control. Not anymore—I made sure of that. Every time I saw him, I'd come up to him and call him a *maricón*, and much worse. I questioned his manhood, that was the biggest thing. When the press conferences came around, I could tell he didn't want to be there. He didn't want to have to deal with me and my attitude. It was all driving him crazy, and while he was busy getting wound up, wanting to destroy me, his fight plan was going out the window. I was psyching him out and setting the perfect trap. Or so I thought. And now we get to the good part . . .

Three days before the bout, I had to get a pre-fight physical, and they connected me to all these machines, including a heart monitor. And here's a surprise. An ECG reveals an abnormal heartbeat. (I couldn't have a heart problem, joked Arcel—I didn't have a heart.) This is what Dr. Bernard Chaitman, a cardiologist at the Montreal Heart Institute, told the media:

> His ECG showed some findings that, in a normal person, might be interpreted as coronary artery disease. This is narrowing of the arteries of the heart. However, this type of ECG pattern is often seen in highly trained athletes. In a well-trained athlete, the heart muscle may be slightly thicker than in an average individual, giving rise to an unusual type of ECG pattern. What happened in Durán's case is his pattern was slightly more marked than in the average boxer.

What bullshit. I was convinced it was a ruse for Leonard to get out of the fight.

Fortunately, Eleta called General Torrijos, and they brought in a famous heart specialist from Panama. I had to take another test. They put me on a treadmill, turned it up to the highest speed, and got me running—*boom! boom! boom!* I kept going, for a whole hour. The specialist looked at the graph and got very excited. There was absolutely nothing wrong with me. He ran off down the hall, shouting, *"Hay pelea!* . . . *Hay pelea!"* We have a fight!

With only a couple of days to go, and since I'd already run an hour on the treadmill, Eleta said there was to be no sparring that day, just to be safe.

And he was right—I was in perfect condition, physically and mentally. I had my family, the people of Panama, and the city of Montreal in my corner. Torrijos did not attend the fight, because his doctor was scared that if I lost, it would be too much for *his* heart. He ended up watching the fight at home on television with his doctor at his side.

This was going to be my first contest as a challenger in eight years and the first time ever in my career I'd enter the ring as an underdog. Leonard was a nine-to-five favorite—even Muhammad Ali had picked him to win. But the sportswriters knew better. In a poll of thirty of them, sixteen picked me to win by a knockout and one to win by a decision. They saw what I saw: Leonard was losing his mind because of me. He lost it again at the weigh-in, flipped me the bird, so I told him to fuck off and called him a *maricón* again. Then I looked at his wife: "Your husband no good," I said to her. "After I beat him, I fuck you." That drove him completely crazy! He didn't know what to do, and he certainly didn't have a fight plan anymore. It was just: Kill Durán! *Perfecto!*

The day of the fight, I went to the barber to have my beard trimmed. I took Chavo, who'd just arrived from Panama. He was only seven, and this was his first big fight. My wife had even made him a pair of boxing shorts like the ones I'd be wearing in the ring: red and white, with ROBERTO DURÁN in big letters.

On the monitor in the dressing room that night, I could see Leonard blowing a kiss to my wife. When Leonard's wife came up, I shot her the bird, and they must have been filming me, too, because it showed up on the live satellite feed in the arena. The fans were laughing their asses off. The scene was set for the biggest upset in boxing history.

"The Fight of the Decade," they were calling it, and there were close to 50,000 people in that arena, including about 2,000 Panamanians, waving national flags everywhere, beating drums. Chavo was with my wife, about ten rows from the ring, wearing his red-and-white shorts. Ringside seats were going for $500. It was also going to be the largest audience in closed-circuit TV history, with 1.5 million fans watching. As I came out with my entourage, Ferdie Pacheco, Ali's doctor, who was doing commentary for the fight, compared the atmosphere to the first Ali–Frazier fight in Madison Square Garden in 1971.

I entered the ring with not only a Panamanian flag but also the white-on-blue fleur-de-lis, the flag of Quebec. The noise was deafening—it was a madhouse. Ray Arcel and Flaco Bala were the first guys in the ring. It had been raining hard in Montreal, and a lot of people wore plastic bags to keep their heads dry. But miraculously, as I bounced into the ring, it stopped: a good omen. The ovation was tremendous, the noise louder than anything I'd ever heard before. I bowed to the crowd, blew kisses to them. There were so many people in my corner in Montreal, yelling, cheering, and praying that I would beat the American Idol. They were booing him! My people weren't here to see Leonard; they were here to see Roberto Durán.

"This is unreal," said Pacheco.

Joe Frazier, who was ringside, was asked by Dave Anderson of *The New York Times* if I reminded him of anyone. "Yeah," said Frazier. "Charles Manson." He was right. You didn't want to be around me before a fight. I was like a caged lion. Now all the waiting was over, we were in the ring, and it was *el momento de la verdad*, the moment of truth.

I was fired up. I warmed up by throwing a bunch of combinations, thinking I'd soon get to do that to Leonard, but those punches would be real, and they'd hurt. Then my idol, Ismael Laguna, came into the ring, wearing a handsome white suit, carrying a little Panamanian flag. We hugged—a beautiful moment for me! What a great night for Panama this was going to be!

Now it was time to take down the American Hero. I was concerned that the referee, Carlos Padilla, might be a problem because Arcel knew he always tried to separate fighters quickly, which would prevent an aggressive fighter like me from working inside. Arcel even approached him before the fight and said, "You're a good referee, but I only hope you let my boy fight his fight inside." I think the pressure got to Padilla, and he really let us fight inside instead of breaking clinches. And that was the plan I'd hatched with Arcel and Freddie Brown, who thought the best way for me to win was to crowd him from the start. "Don't let him do anything!" they kept telling me in training. "Crowd him against the ropes like you did Buchanan": that would allow me to use my counterpunch effectively.

At the start of round one, Leonard came out flat-footed, thinking he could fight and trade punches with me, but he quickly realized I was too much for him. Arcel wanted me to start slow, go five tough rounds, and then wear Leonard down, because he thought a longer fight would be in my favor. There was a lot of feinting in those early rounds, each of us trying to feel the other out. At the same time, I was aggressive, charging him, because that's what had always worked for me—I came to fight, not dance around—and it worked now: I hurt him with a left hook in the second round that staggered him. I got him against the ropes and he held on to save himself, and the crowd went wild—the American Idol already rocking, and I'd only just started on him. I tagged him with a couple more shots and he kept holding on until the end of the round, which suited me fine since I could concentrate on fighting inside him and wearing him down.

"Did Leonard and Dundee make a mistake?" one of the commentators asked Ferdie Pacheco.

"They made only one mistake," Pacheco said. "They signed this fight."

I came back in the third and pounded Leonard hard inside against the ropes. "He's taking some body shots that are going to kill him later on," said Pacheco. In the fourth round, another right drove him back against the ropes, followed by more holding by Leonard. At the end of that round, the commentators asked the former welterweight champion Wilfred Benítez who was going to win. "Durán's not going to win," Benítez said. "Leonard is going to knock him out in the next two rounds. It's an even fight."

Leonard's wife didn't see it that way. She was crying at the end of the round.

I kept leaning on Leonard, pounding him. I cut his right eye, I frustrated him. When I went back to my corner, Arcel screamed at me: "Keep him up against the ropes." As the fight went on, I could hear people screaming, *"Arriba, Cholo!"* I had him—I knew it. Into the eighth round and it was more of the same. By then, Leonard's wife had fainted, which was not surprising since her husband was having the crap beaten out of him.

"What Sugar Ray has taken to the body should have caved in a heavyweight," Pacheco said in the eleventh, and then it was into a wild twelfth round, with both of us trading shots. When the bell rang, I sat down in my corner and told Arcel, "I know I've won. I know I've won."

"But Cholo, you've got to fight two more rounds!"

"Okay, pops. Okay."

Before the start of the next round, I got up from my stool and waved at Leonard to come get some more punishment.

By the fifteenth, he didn't want any more. As we touched gloves, I said, "Fuck you!" and then continued punishing him and playing with him while dodging his punches. In the final second, I tapped my right glove on my chin, mocking him, because he knew as well as I did that the fight was mine.

It took a while for the decision to be announced, and it was a majority: 145–144, 146–144, with the judge from Italy calling a 147–147 draw. I had won the WBC world welterweight title. I jumped up and down, up and down, in jubilation. Pacheco had come in the ring to interview me. "I knew I'd beat him," I told him. "I was more of a man than him. I can take more punches than he can. I'm a better boxer. He never hurt me—he hit me hard, but he never hurt me. I am very strong."

I called Leonard a *maricón* again, grabbed my crotch in front of Benítez and called him a *huevón*, dickhead. He was buddies with Leonard, and I'd gotten it into my mind that he'd been spying on me during training and reporting back to Leonard, though I could never prove it. At the post-fight press conference, he'd call me out: "Roberto! Roberto!" he was shouting. "I want you!" Another *payaso*—I'd get to him later. But right now I didn't care: back in the dressing room, people were all over me, screaming, "Manos de Piedra! . . . Manos de Piedra!" Don King gave me a $1,000 cash bonus, as usual. I'd just beaten Leonard, and Benítez would have to wait his turn.

Leonard walked away with a lot more money, but a lot more pain. He said fighting me was as close to death as a man could come, that he had never felt so much pain from so many punches. His teeth had been hit so hard, he had to push them back into place at the end of each round. A doctor had to go into his dressing room afterward and drain blood from his ears with a hypodermic needle so he wouldn't get cauliflower ears. He said he was thinking about retiring, he didn't need this kind of crap. Maybe Frazier was right. I didn't know who this guy Charles Manson was, but it seemed we both had a passion for inflicting pain.

I won because I made Leonard fight my fight. He was forced to box flat-footed, and that way, I made him take big punches. He thought he was showing a lot of courage by taking so many. Maybe, but mostly what he was showing was a way to lose. "You never fight to a guy's strength," said Angelo Dundee. "You try to offset it and Ray didn't. He tried to out-strong the guy. Durán was being Durán, and Ray was going with him." Dundee was right. I was the superior fighter, physically and mentally. Now the whole world knew that Cholo was champion of the world.

Even the Americans knew their idol had been beaten badly. "It was, from almost the opening salvo, a fight that belonged to Durán," wrote William Nack in *Sports Illustrated*.

> The Panamanian seized the evening and gave it what shape and momentum it had. He took control, attacking and driving Leonard against the ropes, bulling him back, hitting him with lefts and rights to the body as he maneuvered the champion against

the ropes from corner to corner. Always moving forward, he mauled and wrestled Leonard, scoring inside with hooks and rights. For three rounds Durán drove at Sugar Ray with a fury, and there were moments when it seemed the fight could not last five. Unable to get away, unable to counter and unable to slide away to open up the ring, Leonard seemed almost helpless under the assault. Now and then he got loose and countered—left-right-left to Durán's bobbing head—but he missed punches and could not work inside, could not jab, could not mount an offense to keep Durán at bay.

"I admit, he intimidated me," Leonard would say years later. "He knew exactly what to say; how to say it. He got to my head. I tell you he got to my head."

"Many people did not believe I could make it," I told William Nack a few weeks after the fight, "but I did.

Many people believed I was too old to win, but I was not. Many said I could not beat Sugar Ray Leonard. Before the fight I asked myself, 'Why can't I beat him?' I wondered, 'Maybe he's a phantom and you can't beat him.' Maybe they thought I was going to stand in the ring and let him beat on me, like I had my hands tied. . . . That's the only way he can beat me. I would have to be tied to a tree, with my hands behind my back . . . he would have to break me down a thousand times. He was strong, but he did not hurt me. My rage was very big. When I get into the ring to fight, I always give the best.

As a promotion, the fight had done very well, even with nothing like the closed-circuit technology that'd be available today. It made a lot of money, setting a record back then for the highest-grossing fight of all time. It was also really the first-ever "superfight" between boxers in a lower weight division after a decade or more of boxing being all about the heavyweights. It was no longer about Muhammad Ali and Joe Frazier and the other heavyweights, who got all the attention and all the money. Now it was going to be me, Leonard, Thomas Hearns, Aaron Pryor, Marvin Hagler, and Alexis Argüello getting what we deserved. And though people did talk about the others, mostly they talked about me, Durán. Now the whole world knew that El Cholo was champion of the world—they were comparing me to greats like Sugar Ray Robinson, Joe Louis, and Henry Armstrong. I'd never lost a title fight—one win as a welterweight, thirteen wins as a lightweight, with twelve knockouts. No one had ever beaten me for a title—I'd just had to give one of them up because I couldn't make weight. Now I'd become only the third lightweight champion in boxing history to win both lightweight and welterweight titles. Henry Armstrong, Barney Ross— and Roberto Durán. That was it. This was the greatest victory of my career. I'd worked my ass off and now I was on top of the world and ready to party. But I wasn't going to do it alone. I wanted people to share in my success, in the glory of Panama.

For Leonard things were completely different. I'd crushed him, physically and emotionally, and he was ready to retire. He took his wife to Hawaii to get away from everything, but whenever he tried to go for a run along the beach he wouldn't get a hundred yards without having people come up to say, "When are you going to fight Durán again?" and "What *happened* to you in that fight?" and "Ray, you could have won if you'd fought your fight." Every day down on that beach he got madder and madder. By the fifth, he was asking his manager for a rematch, right now. Meanwhile, I was into my fifth day of partying. *Cerveza*, whiskey, women. There would be plenty more days of partying to come.

FIVE

NO MÁS

ARÍSTIDES ROYO SÁNCHEZ may have been the president of Panama, but I was the king. Royo Sánchez wanted me back home right away so I could join in the celebrations that were already under way, and he sent a plane to get me. The streets of Panama had been empty hours before the fight—from around five o'clock, I was told—and of course when I beat Leonard everyone rushed out into the streets again, jumped in their cars, honked their horns. It was carnival time the length of the country. My friends and family celebrated all night. Walla, my lion, was the only one who wasn't excited— he slept through the whole thing.

But I had other plans: *"No comas mierda, Durán—vamos a Nueva York,"* said Victor del Corral. Don't mess around, Durán—let's go to New York. Royo Sánchez was insistent— he wanted my victory to make him look good. There was a colonel who was shitting his pants because I was refusing to go back with him on that plane. "I'm not going back to

Panama without you," he said. "No way am I going to lose my job because of you."

I didn't give a shit about his problems. "Sorry," I said. "I didn't ask anyone to send a plane."

And so off we went to New York. I was no longer that kid who'd been terrified the plane was going to touch the sky-scrapers. I knew my way around the city, and better still, the Latins loved me. Not just the Panamanians; the Cubans, too, the Puerto Ricans, the Mexicans. I'd beaten Leonard, and the Puerto Ricans loved that because Leonard was the guy who'd beaten the crap out of Wilfred Benítez in 1979.

I was having a great time and so was Fula. She went to the Louis Vuitton store and they closed it for her so she could to do her shopping alone. She must have spent $50,000 on suit-cases and clothes. She's just like me—loves bling, stuff that sparkles. She still has all that Louis Vuitton stuff—the suit-cases, the training bag, where I'd stick my passport, boxing gloves, and other gear.

Victor had scheduled a big celebration at his restaurant for me that Saturday night. I went downstairs to the hotel bar to have a drink first and I could see there were hundreds of people outside. I had my drink, thinking how crazy all this was, and when Victor showed up he said, "You need to leave in a limousine." We left by the back way to avoid all those people trying to get a piece of me.

I got hammered that night. There was a big cake topped with the words DURÁN CHAMPION. I signed autographs for everyone even though my right hand was still taped up from the fight. I don't think it had quite sunk in yet how big that victory was. Everywhere we went, for days afterward, people would come up to shake hands.

On Monday, June 23, three days after the fight, I finally agreed to return to Panama with the colonel on the presidential plane. I'd been partying the whole time in New York, and now I was ready to go back to Panama and party some more. The president declared a national holiday in my honor—"Roberto Durán Day"—and nearly two million of my countrymen wanted to celebrate. "Yours is a triumph on a national scale," he said, "and also a victory for the Panamanian people." As the plane came in on its final approach, I looked down and could see the crowds, screaming and cheering. They knew I was coming home to celebrate.

It soon became clear to my family what I meant to the people of Panama. They'd wanted to pick me up at the airport, but there were so many people on the streets there was no way through. The press estimated that as many as 200,000 people had gathered at the airport—as many as had celebrated the previous fall when the United States turned the Canal Zone over to Panama, if not more.

The plane made one last loop over the Bay of Panama before landing. The sea of fans rushed the plane, and I came down the steps, pointing at the belt strapped around my waist. This didn't belong to me, I told everyone: "It belongs to you—my people, the people I love, who supported me!" They went crazy!

The crowds followed our limousine all the way along the

parade route, which took us from the airport to a square out-side the presidential palace. For some reason, there was no carnival queen that year, so they made me the king of the carnival. The float we were on was in the shape of a ring, and we were surrounded by other Panamanian fighters and for-mer champions like Alfonso Frazer and Ernesto Marcel as if they were my court.

It felt like the party went on for weeks. Everybody loved me, but I'd also come to realize by then that I had a lot of fair-weather friends, people who were only too happy to hang off me during the good times but would soon be gone once the party was over. But Victor del Corral was not one of them, and though Panama was my homeland, I felt most at home in New York with Victor in his restaurant, eating a steak he'd cut himself—there was even a steak named after me on the menu. So I decided to leave Panama again and head straight for Vic-tor's Café.

It was now a month after the fight, and we went out drink-ing, dining, and partying with a lot of people. I hung out with my lowlife friends, who never had any money, as well as the millionaires. Night after night, we partied until every-thing was just one big haze. I got to the point where I weighed nearly 200 pounds! But I didn't care—there weren't any more fights to worry about.

Back in Panama again, I needed a break from it all, but there were people actually lining up to get into my house, cars jamming all the streets in the neighborhood, and I didn't mind celebrating with them. It wasn't just one party, it was parties every night, and as many as two hundred, three hundred people in my house. I'd give away money to anyone who asked—as much as $5,000 in an hour.

Eleta seemed to have anticipated all this: he knew from experience that insanity would follow. I was surrounded by witches, he told me. I'd lost control, and things were now moving against me. Nowadays, I can understand what he was talking about.

I've had a lot of *manzanillos* in my life. That's Panamanian slang for people who leech off the rich and famous. The Americans call it an entourage; back then, I called them my friends. It was hard for me to say no to them, because sometimes there were as many as five or six in my camp, sometimes more. I can't recall all their names, but I do remember guys like Ramos and Giovanni who liked to hang with me. Then there were good friends, like Wiwa and Chaparro, and my brothers, especially Pototo—I could never say no to them.

I knew Wiwa and Chaparro from the old days, when we were growing up in El Chorrillo. In the early days, Wiwa was selling lottery tickets there, but as I became famous I started taking him everywhere, especially the United States, because he was always a good guy to have around. When you're a long way from home, it's nice to have family around you to remind you where you've come from. Wiwa went to all my fights, he'd cook for me, and we'd go running together, along with Pototo. In the evenings, after training, we all liked to play dominoes and listen to salsa music. One guy carried my gym bag, another carried my boom box. There was a guy who did my laundry and one who handled security. There was a guy to play dominoes with me and another guy to cook. Yet another guy was there to dry me off. Sometimes they'd fight among themselves to see who could get closest to me, and all the time it was, "Get this for me" or "Give me a hundred dollars." "Okay," I'd say—but then one of them would disappear, or try to steal my car, and I'd have to find yet another *manzanillo* to get it back for me.

Of course I gave all of them money and paid for their food and hotel rooms. I didn't ask a lot of questions, even though I knew they were only along for the ride. I needed them, too, in lots of ways—when I was away, they were the only people I could have a conversation with in my own language, apart from Victor. I guess people might expect me, a *pelao* from the streets, to have been a bit more streetwise. But I didn't see it that way. I had money, they were my friends, and I was glad to help them.

Maybe I do trust people too much. I always see good intentions, never bad ones. But here's the truth: we had a great time! It wasn't just the *manzanillos* around for the fights—it was everyone from my neighborhood in El Cangrejo. Everyone from El Chorrillo—everyone in Panama! My house was full all the time—full to bursting—and occasionally we'd have to put security at the front door to stop any more from coming in.

People were now lining up at my door asking for money— money for rent, college, hospital bills, money to clothe their kids and buy them toys. And I gave it to them—I probably got rid of tens of thousands of dollars like that—maybe as much as $10,000 in a single day. Anything to help poor people, anything to help the people of Panama. Fula told me to stop, because if I ran out of money, there'd be nothing for my family, but I couldn't. I've always been like that—if I have money, then I'm happy to give it away. If I don't, well, I'll find a way to get some. I'm not a philosopher, but I believe that if you're a kind person and love others, the world will love you back. But if you're an asshole, you'll be an asshole all your life and people will only hate you. And when you die, the only people who'll show up at your funeral will be your family. I was in love with Panama, and Panama was in love with me. I was Panama's hero, and I was happy to play that role. Why not? I deserved it. El Cholo was *el campeón del mundo*, and I was going to enjoy every fucking minute.

That's what I thought, anyway, until in September, when I was back in New York, partying, and I got a call from Eleta. "Cholo, we need you in Panama, because we've signed the rematch."

"Don't worry, I'll be back soon."

"No, you've got to come now—you've got a month to get ready. We've signed for a rematch with Leonard for the WBC welterweight title."

"Are you fucking crazy? I weigh nearly 200 pounds! I can't drop all that weight in a month!"

Leonard and his manager, Mike Trainer, had been desperate to get me back in the ring, and Eleta and Don King didn't have a problem putting me in an impossible position—

they had no idea how much of a good time I'd been having. King was in control now; he'd made it a condition of the rematch that Bob Arum wouldn't be involved, because I was the champion now and he wasn't my promoter. Eleta told me he'd asked King to postpone the fight, but King said no way, there was too much money riding on it. I was guaranteed to make $8 million—but only if I fought Leonard in New Orleans in November.

It was news to me that Leonard was even going to fight again. The last I'd heard he'd gone off to Hawaii, talking about retiring. I certainly didn't think I'd be fighting him again, let alone so soon after the first fight. At the very least, I thought I'd have some time to get in shape. There'd been talk of a fight between me and the winner of a Thomas Hearns–Pipino Cuevas match, but that hadn't happened. It would have made a lot more sense for me to have had one fight before I faced Leonard again—a ten-round, non-title fight—but that wasn't going to happen, because everyone wanted to get rich quick.

As soon as I got the call from Eleta, we left New York. But—big mistake—back in Panama I kept partying. Eleta found a doctor to inject me with diuretics to help me lose weight. That wasn't much help—in fact, it drained me and made me weaker, which made the training even harder.

I have never felt as bad as I did then. It was horrendous— all the self-discipline that I'd maintained deserted me after I beat Leonard. I've got two world titles, I said to myself. I've got money, I've got fame—I just want to relax. It happens to

all athletes. You can be great for five, six, seven, ten years—
and then you fall. A boxer is no exception, and for a Latin
boxer, it's even worse: we love to eat and drink and have a
good time. But training is nothing but hard work, all the
time: constant discipline.

People don't understand what it takes to become a champion in boxing. You have to bust your ass every day, every
week, for months on end—and then get up the next morning
and do it all over again. You know what it's like to train for
two or three *months*? You go crazy! It's the most difficult
thing you can ever do. So I'd busted my ass training; now it
was time to go to the disco, *empezar la jodienda, coño!*—start
fucking around. I deserved it! And after the Leonard fight,
that became the norm for me.

Meanwhile, Leonard wanted revenge. He'd heard about
my weight and all the partying, so he wanted to get me in the
ring as soon as possible. He went and found new sparring
partners: nasty fighters. And unlike me, he cut back on his
manzanillos, which he admitted had been a major distraction
with the first fight. He'd had thirty people, maybe more, on
a per diem and still complaining, all kinds of petty shit. Word
would get back to him that one guy hadn't paid his bill. Another was selling T-shirts at the hotel even though they'd
been given the rooms free. It was insulting.

But I wasn't doing the same thing with my *manzanillos*. I
wanted things to be just like they were for the first fight.
"This time, I will kill him," I told reporters. I called Leonard

a clown. When I saw him, I shot him my middle finger, just like old times. "To beat me," I said, "you have to come and fight me. He goes into the ring and tries to imitate Ali, but an imitator is a loser." But it was clear that Leonard wasn't going to let me intimidate him anymore. He was playing his own mind games. He was becoming more of a jerk—more like me.

There was a brief moment of truce. Early on, 7UP had the idea of putting us and our sons in a commercial together. Chavo and Ray Junior hugged each other, each holding a can of 7UP, while we faced off in the gym in street clothes. Then the kids offered each of us a can of 7UP and we looked down at them and smiled.

Leonard was nervous, thinking that I was going to do something crazy. If I acted up, he told them, he was walking away. But I love children—I hugged his son and kissed him. It was a rare moment of kindness between us, and it would be the last for a very long time.

I knew it was going to be a tough fight because of my conditioning. To lose fifty pounds in just a month! *Puta!* A baby could have punched me and it would have felt like a heavyweight, that's how drained I was. I would leave training drained. I felt rotten from the day I started training again, and it stayed that way right up to the day of the fight. A few days before the fight, I saw Leonard running outside the Superdome and I told Plomo, "This guy is going to get away from me."

Arcel tried to keep my spirits up, telling the press I reminded him of Rocky Marciano. "He rips you and tears at you. He might miss a punch, but eventually he'll get you. I worked with Joe Louis fourteen times and before each one of his fights you could look across the ring and see his opponent droop and go to pieces. Believe me, Leonard is going to go in there with some fear in his heart Tuesday night. He's a good fighter, but he knows Durán has him. You wait and see what happens."

There was still bad blood between us, even though this time Leonard was saying some good things about me. The day of the fight, in an interview with Larry Holmes, he said that the first time around he thought I was all hype but now he knew I was for real. Still, he told Holmes: "I don't like him. He definitely doesn't like me. And the reason I don't like him is because he disrespects himself and the public, and I feel that being a champion, you should display class, and he doesn't show class in no shape or form."

Leonard was right about one thing: the dislike was mutual. He was the kind of guy who, if he moved into my neighborhood, would prompt me to move. But deep down, I was worried. I wasn't feeling well. I spent almost every day in the sauna. I went two days without eating. When I stepped on the scale, I weighed 146—I'd lost almost fifty pounds! But it came at a cost: I was too weak—I could feel nothing in my legs. I was nowhere near the fighter I'd been just months earlier.

In the days leading up to the fight, we went through some bullshit with Leonard's trainer, Angelo Dundee, who said my beard was too thick and he wanted it trimmed. Leonard showed up at a workout wearing a long fake beard and a knitted cap, pretending to be me. After his workout, he picked up the microphone and said: "Me no like Roberto Durán. I keel him. Be there." *Que comemierda*. What a dumb-ass.

And then, after the weigh-in at noon the day of the fight, I had two thick sirloin steaks and orange juice at the restaurant in the Hyatt Regency, which is something I'd done a couple of times before to get my energy up. I had a cup of very hot coffee and then a cup of very cold water. *Chuleta!* Damn! That's when the stomachache hit me.

"*Gorda*, my stomach hurts," I told Fula around six. "I don't feel so good." She gave me some pills to make my stomach feel better. But as they were taping my hands, I was still grimacing, and Fula said to herself, I don't like the look of this.

Eleta had seen Leonard, along with his trainers, moving around the ring and loosening the ropes, which was an old trick used to keep an opponent in his place. Angelo Dundee had done the same thing for the Rumble in the Jungle, allowing Muhammad Ali to "rope-a-dope" by leaning back against the ropes to absorb the weight of the punches thrown by George Foreman. "Be careful you don't get up against the ropes," said Eleta. They were doing everything they could to set me up to lose.

Finally, I finished taping up and we headed for the ring. I had a big entourage with me, as many as thirty-six people, including a lot of *manzanillos*, some of whom I barely recognized, all wearing tracksuits and waving little Panamanian flags. Leonard had fewer people, but he did have Ray Charles with him to sing "America the Beautiful" before the fight. Leonard was a big fan because he'd been named after the singer, and he had specifically asked for him, whatever the cost. After singing for some 20,000 people, Ray Charles whispered in his ear, "Kick his ass!"

Years later, Leonard said he had looked me in the eye as Charles was singing, and knew it was going to be a good night. He thought he'd psyched me out already, but I wasn't intimidated by him or the blind guy singing the American's song. I just didn't feel too good, my stomach trouble had been getting worse. Whatever he saw in my eyes had nothing to do with him.

But my record on entering the ring that night was 72–1, with fifty-six KOs. Leonard had those twenty-seven victories, sure, but that one defeat was because of me. I was the better man, the better fighter—that's what history already said. I didn't need Eleta, or anyone, to remind me of it, and now I began to feel better about things and that I could still win.

When the bell rang, Leonard was bouncing, dancing around, from the start. This was a different Leonard from the first fight—boxing this time, not flat-footed as he'd been before. He'd done his homework. At the end of the round, he landed a right; he didn't hurt me, I just smiled. But already I was feeling weaker: there was no way I was going to last fifteen rounds or have the strength to knock him down. I was going to have to find another way out of the fight.

Leonard continued dancing for a couple of rounds, but in the third I got him in the corner and pounded him with some good shots. He smiled, but I knew I'd hurt him. Maybe I could end it early despite my problems? I can do this, I told myself. In the fourth, I continued trying to fight him inside, but he kept holding. Still, I kept on pounding, trying to go to the body. Against the flow of the fight, I knocked Leonard down in the fifth, but they counted it as a slip. I got him again good at the end of the round when he was against the ropes. It was my best round by far, but I'd spent too much energy. During the sixth, Leonard went back to dancing, and in the seventh round he began acting like a clown, moving his head back and forth, taunting me and doing the Ali Shuffle. I motioned to him to come fight me, but he kept dancing. That's not boxing.

Leonard would later say that none of that was planned—he was doing all those things on the spur of the moment—but when he saw I was getting frustrated, he kept going. Of course I was frustrated, because I wanted to box, not dance the salsa with this *payaso*, this clown.

In the eighth, we had an exchange against the ropes, but by then I had had enough. It was not going to be my night. My arms were weak, my body was weak. I couldn't move, couldn't breathe properly. I backed off and waved with my right hand. Leonard hit me a few times, but I kept motioning to the referee that I didn't want to fight.

"What's happening?" said Les Keiter, a TV announcer.

"Durán says no. I think he's quitting. What is he saying, Larry?" he asked Larry Holmes, who was one of the commentators along with Don King.

"He quit!" screamed Keiter. "I think Durán quit! . . . He said, 'No more.' And then he did it again."

"I don't understand it," Holmes kept saying.

And Howard Cosell, the fight commentator for ABC, was yelling: "What? Roberto has quit! Roberto Durán has quit! There can be no other explanation! Pandemonium in the ring, and Roberto Durán has quit!"

I never said, *"No más."* This is the truth. I just turned my back and motioned to the referee that I didn't want to continue. Howard Cosell made that crap up because he didn't like me. When the referee asked me what I was doing, all I said was, *"No sigo,"* I couldn't go on, I couldn't keep fighting. It wasn't my night. I felt like crap . . . but I never said, *"No más."*

Officially, it was a TKO after two minutes and forty-four seconds into the eighth round. Leonard was ahead on all the judges' scorecards, but not by much—by two points on one scorecard and one point on the other two, but he beat me only because of the circumstances. I knew I was a thousand times the better man, that if I'd trained properly, if I hadn't had those two steaks, I would have had him all over again. I didn't have to respect him.

I was the first champion to voluntarily surrender a title since Sonny Liston quit in 1964 against Cassius Clay, and there was controversy that night, too. Liston had been the strong favorite, ten to one, but he went back to his stool after the sixth, spat out his mouthguard, and quit. He'd torn a muscle in his left shoulder and couldn't fight anymore. A doctor confirmed it, but even today people still think that the fight was fixed.

There'd be a lot of commotion that night in New Orleans, too, about whether my fight was fixed. But first, there was a commotion in the ring. Nobody knew what the hell was going on. At ringside, the press people were still trying to figure it out—they could not believe I'd quit. Leonard's brother got in the ring and threatened to fight me, and then the police came into the ring, which didn't really help. In the middle of all this, Leonard came over and hugged me, but I didn't want anything to do with him. I was thinking, I won one, he's won one, so now he has to give me a rematch. So I turned my back on him. I was pissed off, frustrated, out of shape—I knew it was never going to be my night. The whole evening descended into chaos.

Unfortunately, that was just the beginning.

At the press conference later, things started to go bad rather quickly. I said I'd had cramps, that I hadn't been a hundred percent physically or mentally. Leonard may have beaten a legend, I went on, but he hadn't done it by fighting but by trying to shame me—sticking his tongue out and acting like a girl, like a *payaso*—and the longer it had gone on, the more the fans had been laughing. So I'd said, Fuck it, I'm done. I'm done. Hell, my mind was pretty mixed up about the future, too. I told reporters I was retiring. "I've been fighting for a long time. I'm tired of the sport. I don't want to fight any-more." It was all frustration over getting asked questions I didn't want to answer right then.

I'm a proud man, but also an impulsive one. Sometimes I make a bad decision, and in due course, I'm brought up short and think, Oh shit. This was one of those moments—the biggest "Oh shit" moment of my life—but it was too late. I'd let my emotions get the better of me. I didn't know the world would react the way it did, and I didn't know I would get treated like shit for so long. I didn't know it would haunt me for the rest of my life. But it happened. I have no regrets.

But all this was still to come, and having said fuck it, in my suite in the Hyatt Regency, I partied with my family and the *manzanillos* just like I always had. At the time, I wasn't too bothered: it had been a bad night for me—so what? It was only the second time in my career this had happened, and the first since de Jesús had beaten me in 1972, and I'd come back to beat his ass twice. This was not going to be any different. I rea-soned that we were 1–1 with a rematch to come, and then I'd beat his ass because I would train properly, and what's more, I wasn't going to let Eleta dictate the terms of the fight. All I saw was a huge payday and a lot of publicity for a third fight that would show once and for all who was the better man in the ring. I was not going to let that clown humiliate me again.

I wasn't going to retire, of course—I knew that as soon as I'd said it. What the fuck was I going to do, especially on the kind of money I'd earn as a *pelao* who dropped out of school in the third grade? I wasn't going back to El Chorrillo to sell newspapers or dance in the streets like Chaflán. I am Durán. I was going to get back in the ring and kick someone's ass. At least that's what I thought.

My personal physician, Orlando Núñez, had already run tests on me and confirmed my stomach cramps. But all everyone could talk about was *"No más."* It started then and it went on for years. Even now, thirty-six years later, people still bring up that *"No más"* shit. Fuck *"No más."* I'm sick of hearing it, as if I'd had only one fight in my career. What about all the fights I won? What about all the people I knocked on their asses? That's my legacy, just as much as what happened that night. People were quick to forget about that, especially the guys who hung around when times were good. When the shit hit, they soon ran.

I made an impulsive decision, and it went down as infamy in boxing history, with very bad consequences for me. But I couldn't take it back, and I'm not apologizing. It happened, and now I wanted to move on. But obviously, not everyone was ready to.

Me, my family, we were treated like shit. *Mierda.* The state boxing commission fined me $7,500 and threatened to take away my purse of $1.5 million. But they couldn't; it had already been deposited in Panama. Besides, I'd been screwed over once already with the first fight when Leonard made a shitload more money than I did: after all the pay-per-view money came in, he wound up with somewhere between $10 million and $13 million. All I received for beating him was a flat $1.5 million. And now the American writers had the nerve to say that I took the money and ran. "Leonard could not have shamed Durán more thoroughly if he had reached over and pulled down his trunks," wrote Ray Didinger. *Sports Illustrated* wrote that it was "The Big Bellyache." Johnny Carson joked that he'd considered having me on his show to sing "The Twelve Days of Christmas" but decided against it because, he said, "I'm afraid he'll quit by the eighth day."

The worst part was that it wasn't only the Americans who were treating me like shit. When I went to have breakfast the next morning at the hotel coffee shop, everyone around me made themselves scarce, even the guys I trusted most. Ray Arcel was devastated over what I'd done—after the press conference, he'd gone back to his hotel room and cried. He said I needed a psychologist, not a doctor—he'd handled thousands of fighters, he told me, and not one of them had quit. He didn't say so to my face, but I could tell he, too, had lost faith in me.

Eleta didn't even leave me the money for the flight home. He abandoned us like dogs—my pregnant wife as well. One day I was the greatest fighter on the planet; the next, I was sitting in the back of a friend's van with Pototo and his wife, with Fula, Plomo, and "Ratón" (Rat), one of my sparring partners, taking turns at the wheel, driving more than twelve hours from New Orleans to Miami Beach, where my friend paid for me to stay at the DiLido Hotel. I decided the only thing to do was lie low in Miami—at least I felt at home there. Or that's what I thought. Then the shit really started.

Within days, the World Boxing Hall of Fame had revoked my honorary membership. "The World Boxing Hall of Fame is an organization dedicated to the objective of publicly recognizing and honoring the greatest professional boxers in history and highlighting their careers by induction into a permanent place of distinction," its president said. "Roberto Durán's action tarnished the good name of boxing and is a disgrace to all the former champions already inducted into the Hall of Fame."

But my biggest problem wasn't some organization I barely knew. It was my own country. A country that had been solidly behind me now suddenly turned on me. They said I had sold out, that I was a coward, that I had no honor, that I should never be allowed to fight again. They threw rocks at our house and called me a bastard. My mother's home was vandalized with graffiti that read "Durán, Traitor." There was still worse to come. *Gallina*—chicken. *Maricón*—faggot. *Cobarde*—coward. I'd dealt with some pretty rough stuff in my life, but this really tested my mental strength.

Chuleta, things were crazy. I had no idea this kind of shit was going to happen to me. Where was the respect? I'd ask anyone who'd listen. Where were all those people who loved me when I was winning all those fights? *Chupasangre*, we call such people in Panama, bloodsuckers. But I kept quiet because I knew that deep down I was the same man I'd always been. *Al mal tiempo buena cara.* In bad times, keep your chin up.

When things had calmed down, I gave an interview to a Panamanian radio station of Eleta's, stressing that I was not going to retire but instead would seek my revenge against Leonard. I couldn't go home yet—not with everything I was hearing—so I stayed on in Miami and went back to the gym to prove to people that the real Roberto Durán was still here. We spent eight months there, and I was very grateful to the Cubans in Miami for their loyal support.

It wasn't easy on my family. Chavo had kids teasing him at school. He wasn't looking for a fight, but if they wanted one, he wasn't going to hide. You can call me what you like, I can take it. But don't fuck with my family. What do they have to do with it? If people wanted a fight, they should have come and found me.

Of course, it wasn't easy for me, either. When I finally returned to Panama, I didn't go out at all—not like the old days. I stayed indoors so I didn't have to hear all the crap from people who'd partied in my house when I was winning—the same people who'd start crying if their wives punched them in the face. *Pendejos.* Assholes.

Meanwhile, I had serious money troubles. Part of the reason for going back to Panama was to try to cash in on my fights, but there was nothing in the bank. "What money?" said Eleta. "You've spent all your money."

"What money?" I flashed back. "The most I've asked from you has been three or four hundred dollars here and there. What about all the millions I've made?"

"You've been going through ten thousand dollars every month."

I didn't say anything else. I was just really mad. I never bothered to keep track of my money. I made it and gave most of it to my wife to look after. I never saw the contracts or knew what was going on. I didn't know how much I was fighting for; like I said, all I did was sign. My job was to fight, and I trusted Eleta, loved him like a father. And then he turned on me, stabbed me in the back like a traitor, blamed everything on the partying and the *manzanillos*. He said that Arcel was magnificent and Freddie Brown had done all he could. Brown told me that I was not an easy man to handle and he wouldn't train me again unless I changed my lifestyle completely. I thought things were bad when I was hiding out in Miami, but the reality turned out to be much worse!

But what was I supposed to do? The one time I needed them, they forced me into the ring too soon and then blamed me for quitting. What was I supposed to do after beating Leonard in the first fight? Stay at home, go to church every day, not screw around and not drink? That's not who I am.

Thirty-six years later, that fight still bothers me. I still don't want to see that shit: you can watch something a hundred times and you still live it like it's the first time. Recently, Juan Carlos Tapia, a Panamanian journalist, put together a history of my fights on DVD and sent my son Robin the whole set. Robin put a disc in the player and the *"No más"* fight began. "Why is that on?" I started yelling. "Get that shit off my TV!"

Those first months after the fight were some of the worst

of my life. I still had the people who mattered to me—my wife, my kids, my family and friends—but the Durán name was no longer gold in Panama. It was as though everyone had been struck with amnesia and I had to fight through shit to remind them who I really was.

SIX

REDEMPTION

ROAD

IT'S NOT HOW MANY TIMES you get knocked down; it's how many times you get back up.

Everyone thought I was finished except me. Of course Don King was no longer kissing my ass, and he said the best he could do was get me a fight in August 1981 against Nino Gonzalez of Puerto Rico. My purse was $75,000 tax-free, a hundred times less than the last fight against Leonard: shit money, but King didn't give me much choice. Gonzalez wasn't what I wanted, but he was necessary to get to Wilfred Benítez and eventually get my revenge with Leonard. I didn't care about Gonzalez, or any other guy. I only cared about Leonard. Indeed, all the American press wanted to talk about was Leonard. Eight months had gone by and still he didn't want to give me the rematch I deserved. Maybe they should have asked him why.

Arcel was gone—he said he couldn't face seeing me go through all that again—so now it was Carlos "Panama" Lewis in my corner, along with Plomo, of course, who would have walked through fire for me. The fight was set for the Public Auditorium in Cleveland, and it would be televised in the afternoon, about four hours before the start of the Major League Baseball All-Star Game in the stadium there. I had to get down to 154 pounds, the super-middleweight limit, and by July, I was about 165, so making the weight was not going to be a problem. I wasn't going to get caught out again.

I was determined to make it back to the top even though that summer had been very painful for me. Along with all the shit I was having to deal with, I was affected personally by an event with much wider significance. On July 31, 1981, a Panamanian air force plane with General Torrijos on board was flying in bad weather over western Panama, lost control, and went down; the general was killed. It was hard on me because we had so much history together, and I felt I owed much of what I'd achieved to his friendship. I visited his grave and made a pledge: "General, I came here to pay my respects. One thing I will promise: whenever I get my first chance to fight for the championship, I will bring it back to Panama. I will go in as a challenger and come out a champion."

I'd sparred three rounds a while back with Gonzalez— then the welterweight champion of New Jersey—in preparation for the fight against Leonard in Montreal. He'd told reporters he could see my eyes flaming when we sparred, but he said I was a beautiful guy outside the ring. Too bad we weren't going to be outside the ring. I didn't care for him, or any Puerto Rican, and I was going to teach him a lesson he wouldn't forget. At the press conference, he got mad, screaming at me that "a Puerto Rican might go down but he doesn't quit."

I was going to make sure he went down, and I was true to my word that night as I punished him for ten rounds, with good shots to the head, and I had him up against the ropes several times. I could feel I was getting my form back. I won a unanimous decision. What good was beating him, knowing I still wasn't a hundred percent? I hadn't fought in nine months and hadn't been able to put much pressure on him, but my reflexes were good, and so were my moves. The rest would come with training.

Once again, after the fight, things weren't straightforward, as the Cleveland Boxing Commission ruled that my corner had used an illegal substance during the final rounds. After a lot of arguing, they decided it hadn't affected the outcome, so my victory stood, although they did suspend Panama Lewis, Plomo, and Eleta for the rest of the year.

It didn't matter to me: I'd won. I was happy with the way I'd fought, and convinced I would win another championship. I was fixing my sights on Leonard and a rematch. Then there was Wilfred Benítez: *el huevón*—the guy I'd flicked my finger at after the first Leonard fight. I could still remember the look he gave me. Now I was coming after him.

That opportunity would come a few months later in Las Vegas: on January 30, 1982, I'd be lining up against Benítez for the World Boxing Council light-middleweight title. There was a decent amount of time to prepare—none of the rushed bullshit I'd been put through last time. Arcel was now back in my corner, working with Panama Lewis. He now accepted I'd been sick that night, he told me, and no longer doubted me. He'd gone through a rough time himself—for weeks after the fight, he'd hardly slept or eaten—but it had taken him a while to realize he wasn't the only one suffering. When he finally felt better, Arcel had told Eleta to call him if I was ever in a big fight again.

Although Arcel was back, Freddie Brown was out. There had been a falling-out with Eleta, which had nothing to do with me, so I didn't ask any questions. But Eleta was back, so it was almost like the old days. It had taken him some time, almost a year, before he could trust me again—but a condition of him coming back, he told me, was that I had to get rid of all the *manzanillos.*

Before his death, the general had suggested to Eleta that I should train on Coiba, a Pacific island about fifteen miles off the Panamanian coast. It was deserted except for a prison with about 350 inmates; there were sharks in the sea. Eleta had arranged the training site with some prominent boxing officials, and Don King had paid around $25,000 to the government of Panama to convert one of the buildings into a gymnasium. I'd assumed I was going to be back in Los Angeles, which would have suited me just fine. It was only when I was met by an army commander at the airport that I was told there was a change of plan and there was a plane waiting to take us to Coiba.

"Are you crazy?" I said to Eleta.

"No. It will be good for you. You'll be well taken care of."

To fight as a light-middleweight, I had to lose weight, of course, and this would be the ninth time in my career I had to drop down in weight after being at 175 pounds or more. At least the island would help me get in shape: there was nothing to do there except sleep, run, spar, and fish. It was all part of Eleta and Arcel's big plan. They wanted me away from Miami and the Catskills—as far as possible from any distractions.

The trouble was, the guards there treated me like a prisoner, too. They wouldn't let me make phone calls, and even though I slept in separate barracks from the inmates, I didn't sleep well, which meant I didn't train well. I'd brought a bunch of bats and balls with me, as I needed a diversion between training sessions, and I'd play softball with the prisoners, but that just made the guards jealous and they would treat them badly, so that didn't work. Even worse, the guards would eat the food Eleta had arranged for me and my sparring partners—good food, prepared by a Chinese inmate! By the time I left, I was traumatized. All in all, it would have been better if I had gone to Los Angeles—at least that's what I told Eleta.

I got to Vegas a week before the fight and stayed in a private apartment instead of Caesars Palace. Eleta had ordered most of the *manzanillos* out, and Arcel said I was in the best shape, physically and mentally, that I'd been in since I'd knocked out de Jesús four years before. I thought so, too: I was up for beating Benítez. It was my first big fight in a higher weight class of 152½ pounds, and my first big fight since losing to Leonard. All I knew was, I needed to beat Benítez to have another shot at Leonard. I was treating it like my first fight. I had to win. It was as simple as that.

Benítez was good, but not as good as me. He was 42–1–1, one of six fighters ever to hold championships in three divisions, and had won his last title from Britain's Maurice Hope. Like me, he had a reputation for enjoying himself too much and then having to bust his ass to make weight. For this fight, he trained in Puerto Rico with his father, Gregorio, who was now saying I was a dirty fighter, a kickboxer. They were worried, they said, that I was going to use voodoo against him. *Que mierda*. What shit. But he was young—twenty-three, seven years younger than me. I was a nine-to-five underdog.

At the press conference, Benítez's father said they had trained to fight fifteen rounds "just in case you decide not to quit in the eighth."

I laughed. "After I beat Wilfred," I told the reporters, "I am going to get Don King to sign my dad to fight his dad." Benítez didn't like that and he made a move for me. Nothing happened, but it showed he was afraid of me.

"I can promise you this," Arcel told the reporters, "if Durán ever thought he'd do again what he did against Leonard in New Orleans, he'd kill himself first."

On the night of the fight, we came into the ring with some of the guys in my entourage carrying a sign that read "El Cholo: The Legend Is Back."

The game plan was to fight Benítez inside and not let him win the fight on style points. But all night he made himself hard to hit and was quick to the punch. It was a bit frustrating. Whenever I got him against the ropes, he was able to slip me. Leonard was working as a ringside commentator. "I don't see anything in Durán," he said after the third round. I got in a good shot in the fourth—a right—and I got Benítez good again with another right to end the sixth, my best round so far. I felt I had a shot to wear him down—but the strength just wasn't there. My legs started to feel weak, too.

Then in the seventh Benítez landed a right-hand uppercut that drew blood above my left eye, and my corner did well to stop the bleeding before the bell went. I fought hard, like a champion. I never looked like quitting, and the *"No más"* critics had to acknowledge that. But at that higher weight, it was hard to move a man around like I usually could. In the thirteenth round, I got him again with a good right, but I just couldn't sustain the pressure, and as the fight went on, the seven-year age difference started to show, and it was becoming clear to me that, however much smarter I was than my opponent, Benítez was quicker and stronger.

After the bell at the end of the fight, he came over to try to finish with a hug, but I motioned him away with my glove. Then he started to taunt me. *Comemierda.* My people got in the ring and lifted me on their shoulders. We weren't going to back down. The scores were close—145–141, 144–141, 143–142—but not in my favor.

Afterward, Eleta said I should retire. Leonard had offered to fight me again, but only if I beat Benítez, and now he was saying I didn't have it anymore. I was frustrated—pissed off.

I think making the weight with just three weeks to spare had weakened me. I went back to Panama to think over my future. First things first: I had to forget about the fight and have a good time—that had always worked for me.

But the best thing was to get back to boxing. Kirkland Laing was next, in a ten-round super-lightweight fight on September 4, 1982. He was the former welterweight champion of Britain and was a few years younger than me—but I didn't care. I would put my extra ring experience to my advantage. This time, there was no prison training regime: I set up camp at Larry Holmes's gym in Pennsylvania. To show people that I'd regained my self-discipline, I'd go to his nightclubs but not drink.

The fight was a bad night for me, though. I was rusty, had trouble slipping punches, and couldn't get my head moving properly. As I walked out into the ring for each round, I could feel myself standing too upright, which meant I couldn't get my balance or leverage, and so my timing was off. I lost a split decision. It was still only my fourth defeat in seventy-eight fights, but boxing writers were calling it the upset of the year.

Laing beat me because of my poor conditioning, though, not because he was better. I hadn't trained properly—I'd been out at the clubs all night. Even though I hadn't been drinking, it still had an effect.

Now everything blew up. The aftermath was like the Leonard fight all over again. Don King stormed into my dressing room, cussing and screaming, yelling that I had too many *manzanillos* screwing around, making me lose focus, and he was finished with me. Flaco Bala left me. Once again, Eleta abandoned us to pay our own expenses! They all thought I was finished, that I'd never be able to climb the mountain again. The planned title fight against Tony Ayala in November was off the table. Only Plomo stayed loyal.

Eleta told me he was giving up on me because I hadn't trained properly, and he said good-bye by leaving me a million dollars, an apartment, and a house. I was worth more than that, though. But when I asked for more money, he said it had already been spent. I used to just ask Eleta and King for two or three thousand dollars at a time, but he reminded me that even though I'd promised to calm things down, I was still going through close to $10,000 a month on the *manzanillos*, hotels, food . . . It was difficult to give up that kind of stuff, especially when I was so used to it.

It didn't make any sense to me. "But I made so much off this fight," I'd say. He didn't have an answer. The money had gone. I was mad, and I wanted nothing more to do with him. It was a hard place to be. I'm a proud man, and I was suffering inside. I had to take care of my family, and boxing was the only way I knew how.

IN MIAMI, I went to see my good friend Minito Navarro, a famous Cuban sports broadcaster I'd known for years, who'd been the last mayor of San José before the revolution and, like so many other Cuban exiles, left after Fidel Castro took power. We'd first met in 1972, after I'd defeated Ken Buchanan, when Navarro was covering the fight for a Spanish-language radio station in Miami. Now here we were, eleven years later, with Eleta not only having deserted me again but also now insulting me in the Panama press, saying that I was so fat I should fight as a heavyweight. And Arcel was done with me, too.

Navarro was supportive. He agreed Eleta had mismanaged and deceived me. "*Tu no estás liquidado*," Navarro said. You're not finished. "I'll make you champion again—but you have to go back in the gym, have the right diet, and some discipline. You have to stop partying all night."

He was right. I loved the nightlife in Miami. I'd show up with all my *manzanillos* and take over the place, go onstage and sing with the Latin salsa band that played on weekends . . . Now Minito started coming along to keep things under control as much as possible.

Enrique Encinosa, the boxing historian, described Navarro as a Svengali to me. I'd started to train independently, and sometimes Navarro would accompany me on my ten-mile run himself, on his bicycle, and then make me one of my favorite post-workout drinks: two raw eggs in a glass of sweet Spanish red wine.

There would be some other positive influences in my life. I didn't have a contract with anyone to be my manager, but one day a guy named Luis Spada came to me and said, "I'm willing to do anything. I'll even carry your bucket."

"No, sir," I said. "You can be my manager."

Spada was from Argentina and had promoted fights in Panama. For a while, he'd worked with Eleta—that's when I first met him—but had gone his own way. He'd managed the junior flyweight champion Hilario Zapata from Panama, who six days after my loss to Leonard had even dedicated a world title defense to me.

Spada had watched the Laing fight on TV and thought I was lousy, a disgrace. But he wanted to build me back up. He was not a magician, he told me: I was the only one who could change things. If I wasn't up to it, he said, if I couldn't be bothered to train properly, then he was done; he was too old for that kind of hassle. We agreed we'd make it work, but that we would need help.

That's how I found myself in the autumn of 1982 with Fula in Bob Arum's office in New York City. I had gone there wanting him to promote some bigger fights for me and I sat there in tears, hoping he would give me a chance. But Arum and Teddy Brenner, his matchmaker, were skeptical. "What am I going to do with this fucking guy?" Arum said to Brenner. "He's through."

But Brenner convinced him to give me another shot—I was a great fighter, a great attraction. "There's nothing wrong with this guy, physically," he said. "If you get him mentally right, he'd probably beat anybody around."

They were right. "No more rumba," I promised Arum, Navarro, and Spada, "no more girls."

My goal was to win the junior middleweight title by the following June—just eight months away. So they set up a fight for me on November 12, 1982, against another British fighter, Jimmy Batten, on the undercard of the super-fight between Alexis Argüello and Aaron Pryor at the Orange Bowl in Miami. It wasn't much money, $25,000, but at least I was still fighting. But I had my pride, too, and I said no fucking way to the idea of fighting on the undercard—they weren't going to humiliate me like that. So they agreed to promote me as the walkout fighter after the Pryor–Argüello fight.

At 157 pounds, I weighed the heaviest of my career. I also had a back problem a couple of days before the fight and had to go to the hospital for X-rays. Fortunately, I was okay. Although I was not at my best, I still won in a ten-round decision. Arum wasn't happy with the result and told me he didn't think I had anything left. "What am I going to do with him, Teddy?" he kept asking Brenner.

I was training in Los Angeles when Arum came to me saying he had a fight lined up with Pipino Cuevas, the Mexican welterweight. Cuevas had been WBA champion for four years and had hurt people badly, sometimes sending them to the hospital. Then in August 1980 he'd fought Thomas Hearns, and that was another story. Hearns had destroyed him in two rounds. Cuevas had won two of his next three fights since then but hadn't been impressive, and his loss to Roger Stafford had been named "Upset of the Year" by *The Ring* magazine.

But this was a different situation. The promoters knew a fight between Durán and Cuevas in Los Angeles would be a big deal because of the growing Hispanic fan base on the West Coast, not to mention all the Mexicans who'd support Cuevas.

"What weight?" I asked Arum. He told me 152–154.

"No way, I can't make that."

"If you fight him at 154 and beat him," Arum told me, "I promise I can get you a world title fight with Marvin Hagler."

"Well, if that's the case," I said, "fine."

Arum put the fight on in the Sports Arena in Los Angeles and we sold it out, and the closed-circuit venues, too. Arum called it "Super Sábado"—Super Saturday—because the Super Bowl that the gringos love so much was being played the next day. Ahead of the fight, I made a big deal about my Mexican heritage, which appealed to the local crowds, who loved a good fight.

I kept hearing how Cuevas was going to kill me, that I had nothing for him. "He's going to knock you out. He's going to retire you."

I laughed. "I am going to knock him out and turn him into a salad so you can eat him."

Ray Arcel didn't have much faith in me, either—he'd even posted some advice for me in *The New York Times*, though I didn't see it at the time: "Life is like a book. There is a beginning, there is a middle and there has to be an end to the story. And so must a career come to an end. I hope you will see fit to end your career." The night of the fight, he was in

Los Angeles, but he wouldn't be at ringside because he was being inducted by the Maccabi World Union into the Jewish Sports Hall of Fame.

As always, my family came to support me. Fula was very well dressed and would have looked great at ringside, but as usual, once the bell rang she disappeared into the dressing room.

The good thing is, I punished Cuevas. The first two rounds were even, but then I started getting to him with a couple of good lefts. We were both going hard at each other, and it felt good to have my power back. It was going to be a war, and I don't lose wars. At the beginning of the fourth, I hit him with a solid right, and that was the beginning of the end for him. I started pounding him against the ropes and he went down. He survived, but I got him against the ropes again and kept punishing him. He tried to hold and hang on, fouling me, landing low punches. But—*boom!*—I took him down again.

He got up in time, but his corner stopped the fight, which was good for them. All I was going to do was punish him some more. The Mexicans wanted to lynch me, so I stood in the center of the ring and raised my hand as a show of respect and they started to applaud me.

I was jumping up and down for joy—I'd trained well and was ready to go fifteen rounds with Pipino. "This is for my people in Miami!" I told the ring announcer. "I told them I would be champion again!"

Back in the dressing room, I found Fula had locked herself in the bathroom because she was so worried I'd been hurt. When I got into the limousine with Spada, I burst into tears. "I've got it again! I am a hero in Panama again. I can be world champion again."

That opportunity would come with my next fight.

SEVEN

"NO MOORE"

THAT NIGHT I FOUGHT CUEVAS, I wasn't thinking much about a guy named Davey Moore. Why should I? Right then, he was not important to me. But after I beat Cuevas, the situation changed. Moore was a junior middleweight champion in the World Boxing Association, so he had something I wanted: a championship belt. It made sense that we should fight.

The negotiations began with José Sulaimán, president of the World Boxing Council. He loved me so much, he wanted to help me, even though the fight involved another sanctioning body, so he talked to Moore. "If you want to be as great as he is," he said, "you have to fight him and beat him. Then everyone will love you and respect you."

"Who is it?" Moore asked.

"Roberto Durán."

"Let's do it."

Originally, Arum scheduled the fight for Sun City,

Bophuthatswana, in South Africa, as a championship double-header, with WBA lightweight champion Ray Mancini fighting Kenny Bogner. There was a Frank Sinatra concert scheduled for after the fights, too, so Bob Arum decided to call the show "The Chairman and the Champs." But two weeks before the fight, Mancini broke his collarbone and had to pull out; Sinatra was doing the show only because he was a big Mancini fan, so he pulled out, too, which was a shame: that would have been a night to remember. So Arum moved the show to Madison Square Garden.

In the meantime, I went to Washington, D.C., for Bob Hope's eightieth-birthday party at the Kennedy Center, which they were filming for his TV show. The idea had been for "Marvelous" Marvin Hagler to appear on it with Leonard in a pretend fight, with Howard Cosell as the referee. But the day before, Leonard was taken to the hospital with appendicitis, so the TV people had called Arum and asked if they could get Ray Mancini.

"Are you crazy?" said Arum. "Mancini is so much smaller!"

"Well, can you get someone?"

That's when Arum thought of me. I was training in New Jersey, so he put me on a plane to Washington. But Cosell didn't like the idea. "Fuck it," he told the TV people. "I'm not doing it for that quitter." Finally, they convinced him to go through with it. So I found myself in the dressing room, looking at Hagler. "He's not so big," I told Arum and Spada. "Beat Moore, then him next."

The show was great, and there were a lot of famous people there, including President Ronald Reagan, Lucille Ball, George Burns—and Cosell. One of my buddies had brought a skip rope along, so after the show I started jumping rope, and the crowd went wild.

I did meet Frank Sinatra later, at a press conference in Las Vegas. I gave him an autographed glove, and so did Davey Moore. Sinatra told his people that the next time I fought there, he wanted to fix it for me to stay in his penthouse at the hotel. For the first time since the Leonard fight, I felt people were accepting me. If Frank Sinatra was taking me seriously—even wanting me to stay at his penthouse—then everyone else was going to have to as well.

Then Dean Martin dropped by and invited me over to the Sands. He had all this liquor—"Take whatever you want," he said. I think he knew I liked to have a good time and was trying to get me drunk, but I was wiser now and managed to play along with him without touching the booze.

The next morning, someone at the hotel told me he had two bottles of Frank Sinatra's favorite wine for me to take back to Panama. Great, I thought—each bottle was worth $1,000—but I'll save them for the celebrations after I've beaten Moore. It was a nice gesture, though, and showed that these guys understood I was still a legend even after all the mistakes I'd made.

Before we met in Vegas, I didn't know much about Davey Moore. But he was strong, heavily built, and cocky as hell.

He'd started to fight professionally in 1980 and won all of his first eight fights before knocking out Tadashi Mihara in the sixth round in Tokyo for the junior middleweight title. He fought well, and maybe he thought that gave him good reason to be cocky. He thought he had the advantage and behaved as if he had already won the fight. He said he'd watched my fight with Batten in Miami but left after the third round, he was so unimpressed. "Durán was a great lightweight, a good welterweight, and a mediocre junior middleweight," he told reporters. "There's a big difference fighting people at 135 pounds and fighting them at 154. Not only can't he be as physical, he's a lot older now and he's not as strong. I don't think it will be all that tough a fight. He passed his peak a long time ago and I'm still getting close to reaching mine."

From then on, I just saw him as another fighter I was going to punish for being wrong. Forget about those last few fights before Cuevas—I wasn't the same person; even Arum could see that now. I'd worked hard for the Cuevas fight, and I was working even harder for this one. I was taking everything seriously.

Moore was the five-to-one favorite, but his opponents had been nothing compared to what he was up against now. He'd be fighting Durán in New York. I knew from my work in the training camp that I hadn't lost my punching power. As for getting down to the right weight, previously I'd tried to do it too quickly, which had left me weak. This time, my weight had been down around the right level for a while, and I felt very, very strong. This was what I had been like back in the very beginning. I was going to be in the form of my life. I knew right from the start I would beat him.

"I can't find words to express how I failed in the past," I told reporters before the fight. "There are no excuses. Once, I thought I was a man; now I am a man and I know it. In truth, I have such enthusiasm, like it was the first time I came to New York to fight for the title and the people were with me all the time. I've prepared very hard for this. I'm the old lion. I don't fight for the money. I want to show myself that I'm a champion. I do this in search of glory." They loved that—it gave the fight something more than just pitching two men against each other. It was about sealing my place in history.

Even though Davey Moore was a New Yorker, tickets sold slowly at first—because of the Leonard fight, fans still looked on me as a disgraced fighter. Arum met up with a Cuban friend of his who ran a Spanish-language radio station: "How the fuck," he asked, "am I going to sell this fight?"

"Don't waste your money with the American media," the Cuban replied. "Just advertise with the Latin media."

But there was some drama beforehand. I had a friend, Chema Toral, who came to all my fights. I used to give him some of the really expensive tickets, ones that cost $3,000 to $5,000 on the market—two or three for each fight—and he'd come over to my hotel and pick them up so he could take a few friends.

"Eleta wants to come to the fight," he said. "He wants to talk to you."

"No," I said. "I don't want him here. Don't even mention his name."

"But . . . but . . . Let me talk to Mr. Spada."

"We don't want him," Spada told him. "We don't even want to see him."

And that's how it was. I'd known Eleta for nearly fifteen years, but when things got rough, he dumped me, and I never did business with him again.

And then, before we knew it, it was fight night. My son Chavo stayed with me at ringside, but my brother Pototo went back to the dressing room with Fula, praying that everything would go all right. It was the first time he'd been too nervous to watch, although I tried to reassure him that this time I was in control. He didn't believe me and told me he couldn't work my corner. He paced up and down the dressing room, turning the TVs off so he couldn't watch, which was too bad, because he would not have been disappointed.

It turned out that in Panama people were starting to believe in me again: the government closed schools and offices early that day so everyone could watch the fight live on television. I was going to put my name back on the map, and I loved every minute of it. For the first time in a long time, I was enjoying boxing. The date worked out perfectly, too: June 16, 1983—my thirty-second birthday.

The Spanish-language radio station guy had been right. It was a sellout, the first for a fight at Madison Square Garden since Ali–Frazier in 1974, and the gate receipts broke all records for the Garden at the time. There were more than

20,000 people there, and I felt they were all supporting me. Sixteen former and current champions were presented in the ring, including Leonard and Hagler, my idol Ismael Laguna, Jake LaMotta, Ray Mancini, Rocky Graziano, Carmen Basilio, Eusebio Pedroza and Gerry Cooney, Bobby Chacon and Floyd Patterson, Vito Antuofermo and José Torres, and Donald Curry. Arum called it "the return of big-time boxing" to the Garden.

I pounded Moore throughout the fight. I caught his right eye in the first round with a left hook, even though Moore would say it was a thumb. "A lot of thumbs," he'd say later during the post-fight news conference. "Those thumbs were coming from everywhere." But that eye was going to give him trouble, and almost six minutes into the fight, it was closed.

Bam! I kept working him, ripping short blows to the jaw and ribs. He was getting soft and I could feel it. I also felt better than I had in years. Durán was back, I knew it now.

"It looks like a master against a kid with twelve fights," said Gil Clancy, one of the commentators at ringside. "He's taking him apart."

In the seventh, things really went from bad to worse for Moore. With sixteen seconds left in the round, I sent him to the floor with a big overhand right to the face. He managed to get up at nine, but he should have stayed down.

In my excitement, I went to Moore's stool and had to hurry back to my own corner. Moore should have stayed in his corner, too, but his manager allowed him to continue. He later said that he'd discussed stopping the fight in the previous round, but Moore wanted to go on, and they both hoped he would recover and come out of it.

There was no way I was going to let that happen. He was done. "Finish him off now!" Plomo screamed at me before the start of the eighth, and that's exactly what I did. I hit him with a stream of head and body shots and he had nothing in return. I could hear the people screaming for me again—*"Doo-ran! Doo-ran!"*—a chant I hadn't heard in a long while. It was my night. I knew it, the crowd knew it; it was just a matter of time. People were calling for the fight to be stopped, including the New York State Athletic Commissioner, José Torres. Later I heard that Moore's mother and girlfriend had fainted. But the referee, Ernesto Magana, kept things going. "This is disgraceful," said a TV commentator, Tim Ryan. "I cannot understand or condone this referee's activity, and Moore's corner should stop the fight."

I hit him with another right, this one flush to the face. I followed it up with a couple of shots to the body, and he was out on his feet. His corner had seen enough and, with fifty-eight seconds left in the round, threw in a bloodied towel. The entire arena felt like it was going to collapse. The crowd went crazy, chanting, *"Doo-ran, Doo-ran!"* and then singing "Happy Birthday" to me. I got up on the bottom rope and burst into tears.

Arum had made sure that Hagler attended the fight just in case something special happened—and it did. After I won, he brought Marvin into the ring and held up my arm and Marvin's to signal that this would be the next big fight.

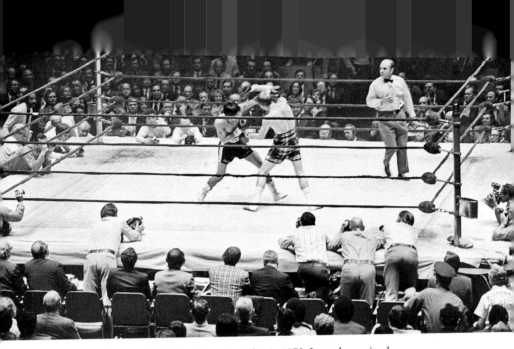

Fighting Ken Buchanan at Madison Square Garden in 1972. I was determined
to beat him and bring home the title for my idol, Ismael Laguna.

Without Freddie Brown (on my left
here), I wouldn't have become the
new world lightweight champion.

At the end of the thirteenth round,
I had Buchanan against the ropes.

Celebrating with Ray Arcel (center) after the Buchanan fight at Madison Square Garden.

Pre-fight physical exams with Esteban de Jesús in 1972. Losing to the then lightweight champion spurred me to win my next forty-one fights.

Goofing around with promoter Don King and Puerto Rican boxer Edwin Viruet before our 1975 fight, which I won in a ten-round unanimous decision.

With my wife, Fula, and our son Roberto Jr., after the Viruet fight.

Throwing a punch against
Juan Medina during the fight
at the Olympic Auditorium,
Los Angeles, in 1973. I won
by TKO in round seven.

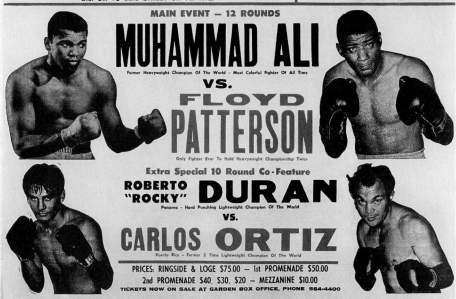

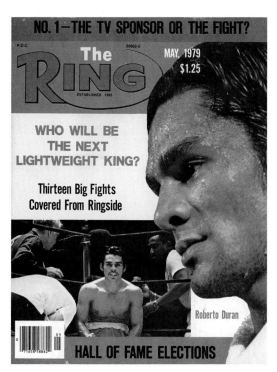

As I became more famous, I'd be listed on the undercard of Muhammad Ali's fights to draw in the crowds and make sure they stayed. Soon I'd be on magazine covers.

Celebrating my wins over
Edwin Viruet in 1977
and Zeferino Gonzales
in 1979.

Americans began calling me "El Diablo." I was the mysterious foreigner fighting their great American hero, Sugar Ray Leonard.

In 1980, I beat Sugar Ray Leonard. Many said I couldn't, but when I got into the ring I could do anything.

Holding my $2,000 bonus after winning the welterweight crown.

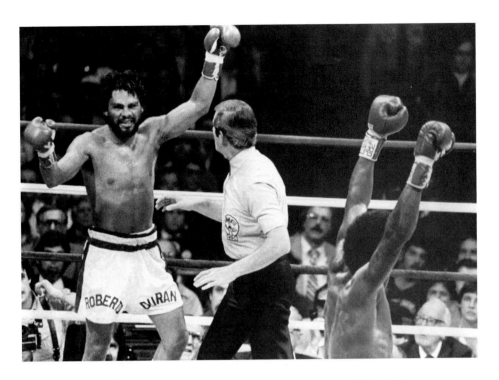

I never said *"No más."* It just wasn't my night, and I couldn't keep fighting.

After tension
and taunting in
the pre-fight,
Don King tries to
separate me from
Wilfred Benítez.

The 1982 light-middleweight bout against Benítez.
In the end, he was better and stronger than I was.

Davey Moore was the favorite in 1983, but I came away with the light-middleweight title.

Marvin Hagler and I did a lot of promotion before our 1983 fight. In the fifth round, I fractured my hand after hitting him in the head and lost by two rounds.

With my son Robin
in Palm Springs.

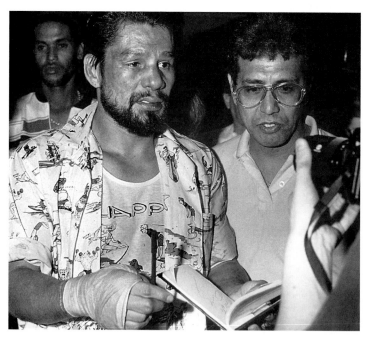

After my defeat to Robbie Sims in 1986. I was determined to keep boxing
despite having lost this fight, the sixth loss of my past thirteen fights.

Training on the speed bag before my 1989 fight against Leonard. Nine years after *"No más,"* I lost our third fight by unanimous decision.

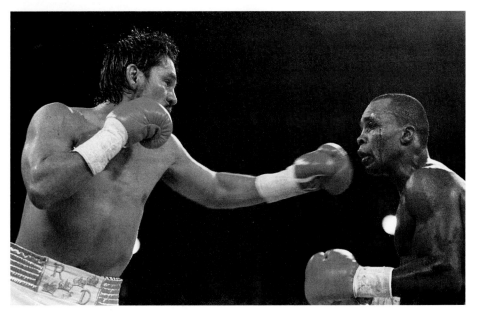

On December 20, 1989, the United States invaded Panama. Many people were left homeless, buildings were destroyed, and my barrio—El Chorrillo—suffered.

At a performance of *City of Angels* on Broadway in 1990.

Fighting Héctor Camacho—the clown—in Atlantic City in 2001. Little did I know this would be my last fight: a few months later I was in a serious car accident.

Meeting Nelson Mandela with Marvin Hagler in 1997. It was a great honor to spend time with such an inspirational leader.

El Diablo. Manos de Piedra. Being inducted into the Nevada Boxing Hall of Fame by Sugar Ray Leonard in 2014.

But I wanted to celebrate this one first. On that night, I joined an elite group that included Bob Fitzsimmons, Henry Armstrong, Tony Canzoneri, Barney Ross, Alexis Argüello, and Wilfred Benítez as three-division champions. I now had the junior middleweight title in addition to the lightweight and welterweight crowns I once held. I earned only $25,000 for that fight, but I was gold again.

"I wanted to prove I could still be champion of the world," I told reporters after the fight. "Not many people believed in me. He didn't seem to be able to handle the infighting. He wasn't as strong. I wasn't thinking this was an easy fight, not as easy as it was."

After the fight, we had to go to a TV show in New York for an interview, and that's when I saw what I had done to Davey Moore. His face was so swollen, it looked like a beach ball. The next time, I told him, "I'll kill you. You'll feel better." There wasn't much he could say, so he just kept quiet.

Of course he soon started coming up with excuses for why he'd lost. He said that a few days before the fight he'd had to have two hours of dental surgery to fix two broken teeth. He'd felt bad after the first round, he said—that his balance was off, that he was seeing "three or four" of me. And he also said he'd had a lot of problems because I'd thumbed him in his right eye. It was all excuses. Not that I cared—I was just there to prove people wrong, to show them I could still fight.

In Panama, everyone went crazy, as you would expect, with cars honking their horns in the streets right through the night—not that anyone was sleeping: they were too busy celebrating. *La Estrella de Panamá* came out with a banner headline that read "Grandiosa Noche de Redención / Durán Reina Nuevamente." Grand Night of Redemption / Durán Reigns Again.

As you can imagine, Roberto Durán wasn't going to go back to his hotel and read a book. We went in a limo to Victor's Café, with people yelling at me, "Look how you hit him!" It was a magical night. I can't remember much about it, but Larry Holmes and Muhammad Ali both turned up. Even my old friend and foe Sugar Ray Leonard showed up to congratulate me and hug me, and told *The New York Times*, "I'm very glad for him."

The next day, there was a news conference in midtown. "I cannot compare this night with any other night," I told the reporters. "This was an exception. When everybody was thinking I was finished, I am world champion again. After last night, I forget whatever happened in the past. I am thinking of the present and the future. I don't remember anything. Last night, I was born again."

A writer from *Sports Illustrated* came to see me at my suite at the Sheraton. I was still buzzing, drinking Moët & Chandon with about fifteen of my friends and family. He put on a tape of the fight and I started to get excited again, throwing punches in the air, the same punches that caught Moore in the face the night before. I was just like a bullfighter in the ring, allowing the blows to come close to me but letting them pass—and Moore was the bull. After the tape was finished, I flashed three fingers in the air: *"Tres títulos."* Three titles. Only seven boxers had won that many and I was one of them. *Chuleta!*

The president of Panama called and arranged to pick us up, and back home there was another parade in my honor. More people turned out for that one than when the Pope came six weeks later—between 300,000 and 400,000. I was back, but it made me laugh that all the people who'd doubted me were back, sucking up to me again. This time, though, I was wiser: I knew that if things went bad again, they'd run. Still, it was party time once more.

Bob Arum came to visit me in Panama, and over dinner I showed him a huge gold ring I'd been given. "How do you like it?" I asked him.

"Muy bonito!" Very pretty.

So I took it off and offered it to him.

"No, gracias, Roberto," said Arum—but I like doing things for people. As I've always said, when I have money, I like to be generous.

Back at my house, I made sure no one touched the Frank Sinatra wine I'd brought back from Vegas. One day, though, after all the partying was over, I went to the bar and found the bottles were empty.

"Who drank these?"

"I did."

It was our cook, a man we called Pechín.

"Chucha tu madre!" I shouted. "You just drank two thou-

sand dollars' worth of wine, you son of a bitch!" He used to drink a lot of my liquor, but I didn't think he'd drink those. That was painful.

About a month later, Arum announced that the fight with Hagler had been set up for the undisputed middleweight championship of the world, the first time I'd be fighting as a middleweight. The press conference in New York was crazy, with about a thousand of my fans there to support me. That was only the start, as Hagler and I got on separate planes for a promotional tour around the country.

It was while we were in Los Angeles that I saw this beautiful car I fell instantly in love with. An Excalibur, a 1984 Studebaker SS four-seater convertible, with a powerful eight-cylinder Corvette engine. An exclusive car—if you wanted to get one today, you'd find almost all of them are in motor museums, in private car collections, or with classic-car enthusiasts: they were rare then, but they're even rarer now. Well, I wanted to be one of those special people who owned one—special people like Frank Sinatra, Dean Martin, Liberace, Sonny Bono, Rod Stewart . . .

I asked Don King for $700,000 so I could buy it. He was startled that I asked for cash, but eventually he gave it to me, and I went straight to the showroom. "That's the one I want!" I said. My wife handed over the cash, and we drove from Palm Springs to Las Vegas in that car. When we were finished in the United States with the Hagler fight, I brought it back to Panama on a plane. It felt good to be loaded again.

We set up camp in Palm Springs, which was hot and dry,

perfect conditions to train in for the fight at Caesars Palace in Vegas. There were more distractions, though, with movie stars and musicians around the place—people like Bo Derek, and Kirk Douglas and his kids, would come and watch me skipping rope and hitting the speed bag. Bo Derek had been in both training camps for weeks, shooting photographs. Most days, she looked like a cowgirl in her western outfit, and one day, after a workout, a reporter asked me if I felt anything for her, because I'd put my arms around her for a picture. Bo Derek might be an 11, not a 10, I told them, but my wife was beautiful, too. Some people think all the celebrity that comes with boxing is a distraction, but I disagree. You can't train all the time, and it was a pleasure to be surrounded by such beautiful people.

Freddie Brown was back as my trainer, and as usual, he wouldn't let me eat when we were training. I had to keep sparring on an empty stomach, dying of hunger while trying to get my body into shape. If it hadn't been for my brother Pototo feeding me slices of bread when Freddie wasn't watching, I would have keeled over long before the fight.

Even though I'd been down this road of strict diet and high-intensity training before, I was still enthusiastic. After the Moore fight, I'd regained my confidence and knew I could go toe to toe with the best. I was sure Hagler was nervous about me.

So were the Petronellis, Pat and Guerino ("Goody"), Hagler's co-managers. They were going to try to influence the choice of referee: they wanted someone to keep an eye on me and, for a start, were accusing me of using my thumbs on Moore and saying I'd hit him in the balls. At the same time, Hagler was calling me a dirty fighter, which told me he was running scared. He was a dirtier fighter than I was; sometimes he used his head like it was his third hand.

Hagler had won thirty-two fights in a row and, it's true, had not lost in almost eight years. He'd had seven title defenses that had lasted only forty rounds, and forty-eight knockouts—but look at the people he'd fought. *Muertos.* Dead people. Caveman Lee. Norberto Cabrera. Tony Sibson. Alan Minter. No one like Roberto Durán. There was no talent in that division, and I was going to show him things he had never seen in the ring. And I knew that Hagler was finally going to feel what it was like to get hit—and hit hard—to the body. We were going to see just how marvelous Marvin Hagler was. The most important thing, of course, was winning my fourth world title.

But it would not be easy. I was sparring in Palm Springs and some guy hit me hard and almost broke my nose. I got a fever and my eyes became swollen and I had to skip training for a week. When I came back, I had to wear special protective headgear. Sugar Ray Leonard came to interview me at the training camp. I put my sunglasses on for the interview, but I lifted them up so he could see how swollen my eyes were. I think the fever took too much speed away from me. These may sound like excuses, but all I needed was a couple more weeks' training. But Luis Spada insisted that I fight, so even though I couldn't breathe very well, I did.

At least coming into the week of the fight, Hagler respected me more than Leonard and Hearns and Benítez had. He told George Kimball, the author of *Four Kings*, that I was a gutsy fighter who'd take on anyone and he admired me for that—the other fighters were all sitting on a fence like vultures, waiting for him to get old. I was never afraid to fight him.

Five days before the fight, Hagler and I were both doing roadwork, running along the golf course by Caesars Palace, when we crossed paths. Hagler ran his way and I ran mine, but we both reacted in the same way and bared our teeth at each other, knowing that in a few days we were going to get it on properly.

Fight night came to Caesars Palace on November 10, 1983. I weighed in at 156½, Hagler was a pound heavier. As I was getting into the ring, Bo Derek got up on the ring apron and said, "Let me see your face," and took a picture. I looked like a movie star, she said. But she wasn't the only celebrity there that night. I remember seeing Michael Jackson at ringside and, behind him, huge numbers of people waving Panamanian flags and screaming, "Durán! Durán!"

I wanted to fight Hagler on the inside, which was always my strength, and from watching his old fights, I knew he was always a little slow getting his hands up. When you boxed him side to side, I realized, he was easy. I was able to block his shots and his arms got tired, but I blocked so many shots that my arms lost power, too. And then in the fifth round I hit him in the head and fractured my right hand. The pain was immediate. The only consolation was that I could tell I had hurt him, as his eye started swelling up badly. I knew I had put him in a bad place, but since I now effectively had to fight him with one hand, I couldn't finish him off. The last round was even, and he was a tough fighter, the kind you could not let up on for one minute; otherwise, he would come at you. It meant you had to use your head to outthink him, and I definitely had him on the ropes.

But I lost by two rounds. I'm still convinced I should have won that fight, because after twelve rounds I was ahead on all scorecards. I won six rounds on two cards and four rounds on the other. But the final card was 144–142, 146–145, and 144–143, all in favor of Hagler. It was the first time he'd had to go the distance to defend his title. *Chuleta!* If only I hadn't fractured my hand! After the fight, I took my gloves off; my right hand was swollen. I went to a doctor to have a cast put on it. "How did you fight like that?" asked the doctor.

"I wanted to tear his head off," I told him. It hurt like hell, and when Bob Arum tried to shake my right hand, I winced and offered my left. I had to keep it in a cast for three weeks.

At least I'd earned the respect of the American writers, and all the fans who kept bringing up the second fight with Leonard. "Durán erased [the] term of cowardice from Panama's Spanish dictionary," wrote Will Grimsley of the Associated Press. It was also a good night for me financially, as my payday was a cool $6 million. Hagler got about $10 million, and he earned every penny. "That man's a legend," he said after the fight. And of course I still had my World Boxing

Association junior middleweight title, because that belt was not on the line.

It was a shame I never had a rematch with Hagler, because I deserved it. I couldn't stop thinking that if I hadn't fractured my hand and had beaten Hagler, I would have fought Juan "Martillo" (Hammer) Roldán, the middleweight from Argentina, who ended up fighting Hagler in 1984 instead. That could have been millions of dollars for me. And a fight against Eddie Mustafa Muhammad, a bunch more millions. But they ignored me, and they ignored Spada, who agreed that we deserved a rematch.

But another big fight came from that night. After the decision was announced, I looked down at Leonard, who was ringside, wearing a tuxedo, doing commentary on the fight. "You can beat Hagler," I said.

"Why are you telling me that?"

"Because you're in the gym every day, I'm not. I only went to the gym to train for this guy. You'll beat him."

"You sure?"

"Yes—all you have to do is box him."

And that's exactly what happened when they fought in 1987. Leonard beat him, even though it was a close fight and a split decision. He could have beaten him more easily if he hadn't spent so much time on the road running.

Much later, I heard that Hagler was back in the gym three days after the fight. Me? I partied for three days straight with my hand in a cast. But this is who I am, and I'm not going to apologize for living my life. It didn't matter that my skills were deteriorating as my career went on, and it was true that my body couldn't take the punishment as it once had: if there was good money offered, I would chase it.

Although I lost to Hagler, I would finally get a big consolation prize. A few months after the Hagler fight, I was in a nightclub in Miami with a couple of women when Spada showed up with a Cuban guy, Walter Alvarez. "This gentleman," he told me, "wants you to fight with Tommy Hearns." It's crazy now to think that this is how fights used to get made!

Alvarez told me he was going to offer me such-and-such.

"How much? Bring me half a million dollars and I'll fight him."

"Are you crazy? Where the hell am I going to get half a million dollars at eleven o'clock at night?"

I told him as far as I was concerned tomorrow didn't exist: it was half a million.

"Forget it," I said to one of the Cuban women. "We'll never see him again"—and I kept drinking my whiskey. An hour goes by; two hours.

Then, around three a.m., Alvarez reappears. "Look, Durán—I couldn't get the money. I've been talking to my friends, but it's hard to come by. But I was able to get together a quarter of a million." He had it in a suitcase and asked me to count it.

I didn't have to: I told him his word was good enough for

me. I handed over the money to Spada and said, "Okay, we'll talk tomorrow." Then I told the girls the party was starting.

It turned out they were lesbians and around dawn, when I was thinking it was time to call it a night, one of them suggested a threesome. But with all the drinking, I got on top of the wrong one; she got all angry with me and spoiled what should have been a great way to end the night.

Now I suddenly had a huge amount of cash, however—more than I'd ever had at one time. What a mistake that was! For the next two and a half weeks, I had the best time of my life, burning through thousands of dollars, going from one club to another. It went on so long that, by the end of it, I'd almost forgotten about the Hearns fight, and it was only when Spada sat me down and told me how we were going to do the training that I got on the scale and realized I now weighed almost 200 pounds!

But the contract was signed, and I was due to fly out to the Bahamas to train. I had one month to make weight. Here we go again, I thought. Shedding the pounds had always been my problem, but this was harder than ever. I went days without eating, and had to do things like sitting in a hot tub, sucking lemons, to sweat off as many pounds as possible. I was dehydrated all the time, but I wasn't allowed to drink and eventually resorted to letting the water run into my mouth when I was taking a shower but not swallowing it.

All this was long before training began to be planned based on scientific principles; I was just doing things I'd learned in the gym back home. I had no idea what kind of damage I was doing to myself, but I didn't care as long as it worked—though I could feel my muscles getting weaker, not stronger.

My family came to visit me at the camp even though my son Robin was only three. It was good to have them around, but there were times when I was in that hot tub, sweating like an animal, and the kids would come in and start screaming, "Daddy! Daddy!" and the noise really got to me. "Fula, please take the kids away," I said. "I can't deal with them right now."

That was when Fula knew I was going to lose. She just hoped it would be by a decision. I hope he isn't hurt, or killed, she was thinking. Later, Robin would tell me that he knew, too, even as a little kid, something was wrong and I was going to lose that fight. To this day, he says it is the saddest memory he has of my days as a fighter. As for me, I'd been through this all before and couldn't tell the difference, but it did seem that everyone was expecting me to lose. My old friend Navarro would have nothing to do with me. "Hearns is younger than you," he told me. "He's stronger, and he's a better fighter than you. He'll knock you out in the third round. I will not go back in your corner."

I'd heard all this sort of shit before, but I can see now that everyone was right. Just to get in the ring was like going through hell. Losing the last three pounds was horrible, like shedding blood, and I barely made it, arriving at the weigh-in at 153¼. After all that, what I needed was a break, not a fight that people were describing as the hardest of my career.

Caesars Palace in Las Vegas was as hot as hell, maybe ninety degrees. Training in the Bahamas was supposed to condition me for the heat, but this was crazy. It was June 15, 1984, the day before my thirty-third birthday, but this wasn't the birthday present I'd hoped for.

From the start, things didn't go my way. About a minute into the fight Hearns got me on the ropes. He tagged me in my right ear; I wriggled out, got back to the middle of the ring, but then he tagged me with a right. He hit me in the head and drew blood under my left eyelid. This was definitely not the plan I'd been working on. When I hit the canvas in the middle of that first round, what came into my mind was those two lesbians in Miami—I don't know why, but it made me laugh. I tried to shake that out of my head and got up quickly. Then Hearns got me up against the ropes again and knocked me down with a flurry before the bell rang. I was in a bit of a haze and ended up going to the neutral corner. Jesus—there were still fourteen rounds to get through if I didn't want to get KO'd. Maybe people were right, I thought.

From the moment the bell rang at the start of the second, Hearns got me up against the ropes again. I waited and waited for a break to be able to push him away and start boxing and that's when he faked a left to the body and finally popped me with a big right hand—*boom!* I went down right on my cheekbone and that was it. *Bing, bang, bing, bang*—he'd knocked me out and I couldn't get up. I was paying for the consequences of fucking around too much—it was all the fault of those lesbians! When Fula heard I'd been knocked out, she started screaming, "No, no! I don't want to know!"

Hearns became the first man to knock me out, but it had taken eighty-three fights before it happened. He knew what he'd done was special, and later said he'd been fighting a legend, the greatest man he'd ever faced. Although no one believed me, I still think if I'd lasted a few more rounds, I would have beaten him. As it was, I got frustrated by all the questions and when I got back to Panama I told reporters at the press conference at the airport that I was retiring. I didn't want to think about boxing anymore. I didn't want to live in the past. "I'm thinking now about having fun," I told them. "Good, clean fun."

It was a relief to tell the world that I was done with boxing. I had money in the bank and could look after my family, which is why I'd gotten into the ring in the first place all those years ago. I had done everything I had wanted to. I felt I was born again. Whatever had happened in the past, I was going to leave it there and get on with the rest of my life.

EIGHT

EL CAMPEÓN

There was more to life than boxing. Back in Panama, we reunited the salsa band, which hadn't played since the mid-1970s. This time, we called it Orquesta Felicidad, in honor of my wife. My brother Pototo was back in it again, as well as my friend Marcos and a few others. We toured the country with a few guest appearances, including, believe it or not, Wilfred Benítez, who played timbales. "We were rivals in the ring but not in music," he said when he asked to join us. I couldn't disagree with that.

We recorded another LP and released a single, "Pa la Calle a Echa un Pie," on which I sang lead vocals. I also played the *güiro*, a Latin American percussion instrument made out of a hollow gourd. I was not the best singer, I knew, but I was good for business, and everywhere we went the fans loved us, particularly when we toured outside Panama. We went to Venezuela, Colombia, El Salvador, Las Vegas, Los Angeles, New York, and Miami, but one of our most memorable trips was eight days in the Dominican Republic for Carnival, touring the entire island.

My fame also got me a part in *Miami Vice*, on an episode that first aired in 1986. I didn't play a boxer: I was a drug dealer called Jesús Moroto who gets busted. Frank Zappa was in the same episode. In the script, Don Johnson, who played Crockett, comes to see me in prison.

My line goes: "It takes a tough cop to bust me, Crockett."

"You got thirty seconds, before I walk out of here," Crockett tells me. "Now, what did you want me for?"

"Payback!" I say, and reach over and kiss him on the cheek. Then I pull a makeshift gun from the back of my pants: "We find out how tough you are." And I shoot myself.

A few years later, I got a cameo role in the movie *Harlem Nights*, with Eddie Murphy and Richard Pryor. I said to Pryor's character, "You wanna kick he ass?" I wasn't much of an actor, but these little parts were well paid and good fun.

I also went back to driving my fast cars and flying my microlights. I'd seen these planes up in the sky and said to myself, "*Chuleta*. I have to learn how to fly."

One Sunday after I'd gotten my license, I went up in my microlight and forgot to maintain the proper speed once I got to altitude. I was going too fast and quickly losing control, and before I knew it, I was heading toward the Puente de las Américas. The higher I flew, the more scared I became, and I forgot all the things my instructor had told me—all I could think about was that I was going to crash badly. I changed direction and headed toward the sea, thinking it was safer to ditch in the water than get wrapped around a tree. I was still coming in too fast, and when the aircraft hit the water, there was a huge bang and then everything went dark and blurry. I was trapped in the cockpit, and the whole time the plane was sinking. I asked God for help. I lashed out and—*bam!*—was able to free myself, bob up to the surface, and start swimming. A fishing boat dragged me on board, but the tail of the plane slipped out of our hands and we lost it. When I explained to Fula what had happened, she said it had been a crazy idea for me to learn to fly, and showing up soaking wet after crashing didn't convince her otherwise.

Needless to say, enjoying myself like this, I was going through huge amounts of money. One of my friends told a reporter I was spending $8,000 a week. I never kept count, but it wouldn't surprise me—we were too busy having a good time! With the band, the flying, and the family, I didn't think about boxing ever—didn't even watch it. I didn't fight at all in 1985—didn't even bother watching Hagler destroy Hearns in Las Vegas in April.

Soon enough, the money started running out, but mostly I was getting bored and restless. At the end of 1985 I went back to the gym and started hitting the bags. To start with, it was just to pass the time, but after a while I got back in the ring and started sparring again. I didn't worry about the weight or speed work, but it was good to feel that I could still move my feet properly, that I could still react when someone went for me.

One evening I sat down with Fula and told her I wanted

to box again. She'd seen it coming, and although she wasn't happy, she knew it made sense—it would keep me out of the house and stop me from bothering her and it would bring in some money again. Rumors were going around that I was broke, and it was true that times were bad, but I wasn't penniless. I still had property, six cars, and lots of jewelry, but I would have hated to sell that stuff off—it was the last remnants of my boxing legacy.

My beloved Excalibur was not one of those cars, though, and giving it up had been the most painful decision of my life. I'd had to sell it at a discount to some guy in Panama. What could I do? I needed *plata*. Money. The answer was to go back to the only thing I knew—fighting.

I didn't make a big announcement about coming out of retirement since I didn't know how long it would last, and when I finally came back, in January 1986, the competition wasn't much. I beat two guys in Panama, both by knockout, but nobody seemed impressed, even though one of them, Manuel Zambrano, was the Colombian junior middleweight champion. I dropped him with a left to the jaw in the second round. It felt good to do that in front of 16,000 of my people at the new Panama Gymnasium.

Bob Arum had promised me that if I won, I'd fight the winner of the John Collins–Robbie Sims middleweight fight, but I was still obsessing about a rematch with Hagler. I even said I was ready to take on anyone in his family—except his parents—to get to him and win another championship.

Instead, I took on Sims on June 23 in Las Vegas as part of a card called the "Triple Hitter," which included Barry Mc-Guigan and Hearns defending their titles. I was now 79–6–0, with sixty knockouts. "I'm not washed up," I told reporters. "I want that fourth title."

It didn't go well against Sims: I lost a split decision. Afterward, I said I wanted to continue fighting, but I had now lost six of my last thirteen fights. And that's when I connected with Luis de Cubas.

"Oh, you're going to be my manager, are you?" I said when we met at Miami Airport. "Give me a hundred dollars, then." That's how bad things had gotten.

De Cubas had arrived in Minneapolis from Cuba in 1966 when he was nine. Now he was living in Miami, working at a bank in Miami Beach and trying to get into boxing promotion with Chris Dundee, Angelo's brother. He gave me the $100 and put me up in a hotel in Coral Gables, just outside Miami, where he was friends with the owner, and they allowed me to stay there until he could put a fight on for me and pay me.

The first was at the Miami Beach Convention Center, and de Cubas said I was guaranteed $15,000 and a cut of the gate. I was going to fight José "Pepe" Quiñones, who had just knocked out Doug DeWitt. But three weeks before the fight, Teddy Brenner called de Cubas, saying Quiñones had a rematch clause. That's when Victor Claudio, a Puerto Rican, came into the picture.

We filled the Convention Center with the help of Chris Dundee, who was a great promoter—he'd do wrestling shows in Miami every Wednesday night and pack people in with American wrestlers the fans loved, like Ric Flair and Hulk Hogan.

I beat Claudio by a decision. I took home $15,000, maybe $20,000, but no one picked up the TV rights for the fight.

Besides a new promoter, I got a new manager as well. Carlos Hibbard was from Panama, an unemployed cabdriver and amateur nutritionist. Like me, he was a street kid and we had a lot in common. We'd originally met in New York, he reminded me, just before I fought Davey Moore, when he'd asked me for my autograph.

In 1987, Hibbard went to the nightclub in New York where I was playing with Orquesta Felicidad. He took one look at me and must have thought, "You don't look anything like a boxer." I weighed 218 pounds then. But he thought he could get me back in shape. "I want to see if you have anything left," he told me. He said that I still had the reflexes and all I needed to do was adopt the weight-loss program he'd devised. So now we were working together!

He had to borrow money to get to Miami to be able to do so, but somehow he did it, and he put me on this strange diet that included herbal teas and a tonic made up of ginseng, peppermint, and fermented garlic. It was weird, but that shit worked.

After I beat Claudio, the next guy up was Juan Carlos Giménez. "Durán, you can beat this guy?" de Cubas asked me. Although he was ranked seventh in the world then, and a big guy, Giménez was very beatable. That's the kind of fighter de Cubas wanted in front of me. He didn't have the money to make it happen, but he hooked up with Willy Martinez, who had founded Ivette Promotions. De Cubas also represented the heavyweight José Ribalta, who'd just gone ten rounds with Tyson, so they wanted both of us on the card to fill the seats.

The Convention Center in Miami wasn't available, so they took the fight over to the Hyatt downtown, in front of 5,000 people. De Cubas had a tape of Giménez he wanted to show me, and after looking everywhere, he found me partying at a nightclub called Rich and Famous. He managed to drag me out, and we sat down in the manager's office. I watched the tape for maybe fifteen seconds. "Oh, get me this guy," I told him right away. "I'll kill him."

The day of the fight, I showed up at the weigh-in in a limousine even though most people had written me off. I'd been having bad headaches, and when the doctor checked me out he found I had high blood pressure, so we had to wait for it to go down before he'd sign off that I was fit to fight. De Cubas was very worried: the fight was sold out. I asked him what he thought of Giménez.

"Don't worry, Durán. Juan Carlos is a *palomita*." A little dove.

I got hit hard with a right first round but fought my way out. Giménez thought I was in trouble, but I wasn't really, although I still had a headache and couldn't move all that well. But as the fight went on, my headache got better and I was able to think more clearly. I could have knocked him out, but I didn't dare overdo it. So by the time we got to the fifth round and he was still standing, I looked over at de Cubas and said, *"Palomita, eh? Palomita?"*

That fight took more out of me than I was expecting, but I still won easily by a decision: the first round was the only one he won. It was just as well that I did, because Willy Martinez paid me $50,000 for it, which I badly needed to keep the family going.

De Cubas still needed more cash, so he brought in a business partner, Mike Acri, who was connected to Jeff Levine, another promoter, and we went to New York to make a deal for a fight against Ricky Stackhouse, a rising prospect with a 19–4 record and ten knockouts. Levine gave me my $50,000 in cash in a nylon bag and I signed on the spot.

I asked de Cubas to take me to this Dominican guy's place that sold beautiful crocodile-skin shoes, and I walked out with seven pairs, including some with fur lining, just the way I like them. I didn't tell Fula, since I spent $15,000 to $20,000 that day.

Years later, Luis Gardini, who owned the shoe shop, fell on hard times and came to me, asking to borrow $30,000 or $40,000 to get himself back on his feet again. I loved his shop so much, I gave him the money without getting anything on paper. "When I get this turned around, Durán, I'll pay you back," he said. But I never heard from him again.

I fought Stackhouse in Atlantic City's Convention Center and won a ten-round decision, and then I fought a guy named Paul Thorn at the Tropicana Casino, also in Atlantic City, and beat him by TKO in the sixth. I cut him up pretty bad, above both eyes, while his mouth was bleeding all over the place, but he cut me, too, over my left eye, with a head butt, and we ended up having to go to the hospital in an ambulance together.

I think Thorn was the only fighter to go on to write a song about me. It was called "Hammer and Nail," and it told the story of our fight, how when we got into the ring my "punches began to rain down" on him. Finally Thorn's corner called it quits. Why did I knock him out like that? As he wrote in the song, I'd "rather be a hammer than a nail."

Yes, I was a hammer, and I needed bigger nails, bigger fights.

A few months later, in Atlantic City, I met another of the great boxers: Mike Tyson.

At the time, Tyson was the king of boxing. He'd knocked out Larry Holmes in Atlantic City. He'd crushed Tony Tubbs in Japan. Now, in June 1988, he was fighting Michael Spinks in Atlantic City at the Trump Plaza. De Cubas had taken José Ribalta with him because he was trying to get a rematch with Tyson through Don King, and he was also trying to get tickets for me and Ribalta for the Tyson fight. He'd asked King for a ticket for me, but with the bad blood between us, King said no. Then de Cubas ran into Steve Lott, Tyson's assistant manager. "Steve, I'm really embarrassed," he started saying, "but I got Durán coming in for the fight and I don't have a—"

"Louie, please," said Lott. "He's Mike's idol. He loves Durán!"

In his memoir, Tyson said this about me:

> A lot of people assume that [Muhammad] Ali was my favorite boxer. But I have to say it was Roberto Durán. I always looked at Ali as being handsome and articulate. And I was short and ugly and I had a speech impediment. When I saw Durán fight, he was just a street guy. He'd say stuff to his opponents like, "Suck my fucking dick, you motherfucker. Next time you're going to the fucking morgue." After he beat Sugar Ray Leonard in that first fight, he went over to where Wilfred Benítez was sitting and he said, "Fuck you. You don't have the heart or the balls to fight me."
>
> *Man, this guy is me,* I thought. That was what I wanted to do. He was not ashamed of being who he was. I related to him as a human being. As my career progressed and people started praising me for being a savage, I knew that being called an animal was the highest praise I could receive from someone. I was sad

when Durán quit during the No Más rematch with Leonard. Cus [D'Amato, Tyson's manager] and I watched that fight in Albany and I was so mad that I cried. But Cus had called it. "He's not going to do it a second time," he predicted.

And Tyson told me that when I fought Davey Moore, he'd snuck into Madison Square Garden, pretending he was me, and up to the gallery. Tyson was just a kid then, only sixteen, a nobody, but he was fanatical about me. Later he told me he spent hours at home shadowboxing, screaming, "Durán! Durán! Durán!" So getting a ticket was not going to be a problem.

"When I tell him, Mike's going to be so happy," Lott told de Cubas. "The only thing is that Mike might want to see him."

So we went to the Seacoast Towers to see Tyson, who was staying in the penthouse. He had been sleeping and came out wearing only a Diet Pepsi towel, which he had to do as part of his endorsement deal. He came and gave me a huge hug. He knew I was a badass, and he wanted to be one, too.

Then he went crazy, dancing around the room, shouting, "Roberto Durán! Roberto Durán! Oh, Roberto! Roberto!" He told me, with de Cubas translating, "I feel like a girl who has fallen in love for the first time."

Eventually, he sat down and started talking about my

fights; later he'd say that his favorite fight of all time was my first fight with Leonard. He could remember all the details, including the exact dates. "How could Alexis Argüello say he could beat you, when he lost to Ñato Marcel and you beat Ñato Marcel?" He was a real obsessive about the sport, and it was easy to see he was going to be one of the best boxers around.

Tyson said he felt bad he couldn't give me tickets for the first row, but he had some for the fourth. He asked if I could come by the dressing room before the fight, and then he asked my advice on what he should do in this fight.

"Hit him low. He has a left foot a little messed up, so hit him on that side. Mike, you're a lot stronger, bigger. Jump on him."

And then Tyson goes and knocks him out in ninety seconds without breaking into a sweat! Later he told Larry Merchant of HBO that it was me who told him what to do.

After the fight, we went to the dressing room, and of course there were a ton of celebrities outside, but none of them was allowed in except me. Tyson was standing there in a towel with his then wife, Robin Givens. He was so happy to see me and told de Cubas that if he hadn't promised his gloves to the Boxing Hall of Fame, he would have wanted to give them to me. "I hit him just like you told me!" he said. "Why don't you come to the party Don King's throwing for me?"

Don King was the last person I wanted to see, but it didn't

matter—there were hundreds of people there. I saw Gregory Hines, the dancer. And sitting on a throne, with a crown on his head and a fancy cane in his hand, Mike Tyson, the undisputed king of boxing. I took some photos with him, drank some champagne—all of which gave me back a taste for life at the top that I'd once enjoyed so much. What I needed was another title.

Iran Barkley was on the radar—a rising American boxer from Brooklyn who'd just destroyed Thomas Hearns in June in a three-round knockout to win the WBC middleweight title. A Cuban-Lebanese guy, a friend of José Sulaimán, reached out to Barkley to see if we could make the fight. They went to Stan Hoffman, Barkley's manager, with a tape of my fights and urged him to give me the opportunity to become the only Latin fighter to win four world championships in four different weight classes. I wanted it so much, I could almost taste it. Finally, I got the news: February 24, 1989, in Atlantic City.

I'm sure they thought I was easy pickings, and an opportunity for Barkley to make a name for himself by picking off a washed-up legend, especially when they saw me at the first press conference, when I weighed 227 pounds, more than I'd ever weighed before. We were going to fight at 160 . . . Here we go again, I thought: seventy pounds to lose in two and a half months. De Cubas told me to get to Miami—"I have everything here for you," he said. "Gym, sparring partners, whatever you need."

I lived with a couple of friends in an apartment off Biscayne Boulevard. My old friend Wiwa ran with me, cooked for me, too, even bought the groceries. Giovanni, Chaparro, Ramos, and the other *manzanillos* were there, but they only wanted to party, and I tried to ignore them as much as I could. I trained well for that fight over at Caron's gym, in a Dominican neighborhood, although de Cubas sent me some monsters as sparring partners and, by the end, the training sessions were more like real fights. One of them got so upset at me hitting him that he quit.

I went running three times a day in the park next door, wearing army boots. Sometimes I could only manage to run very slowly, but as the days and weeks went by, the weight came off. Right until the day we left for Atlantic City, I kept running with those boots on, and I'd run so much around the park, I'd worn the grass out, leaving a trail behind. I never wanted to set foot in that park again.

I cried, I was so mad. People were saying the New Jersey Boxing Commission was crazy for letting me fight Barkley. He was nine years younger than me and much bigger— six-one, whereas I was only five-seven—and he had a 25–4 record, with sixteen knockouts. Growing up in New York, he'd been in a street gang, so I guess everyone thought he was tough shit, someone who could impose his will on me. Fuck that. Not me. So many people were against me, on the radio and in the newspapers, and most of them were Panamanian. I prayed while I ran in the morning for God to give me the strength to shut those people up.

It was crazy back in Panama, too. "Don't let your father fight," people would say to Robin, who was now eight. "He's going to get himself killed." His schoolteachers gave him letters for me that went, "Durán, you have a family. You live for your kids. Don't leave those kids orphans." The newspapers picked up on it and word got out pretty quickly. "He's past his prime. He's an old guy." Even those in my corner had doubts. "You have to box him," de Cubas kept telling me. "You can't stand toe to toe with him. He hits too hard. He's too strong."

Then came the snow. On fight night, the Atlantic City area got twenty-seven inches. It had been Fula's birthday the day before and she'd taken the kids to the boardwalk to relax, but on the way back to the hotel they got caught in a snowstorm and had to take shelter for a while in the lobby of another hotel. When they made it back to Trump Plaza, it was very emotional in the dressing room. Donald Trump came in to say hi to me. My kids were nervous, watching me get my hands wrapped. And Robin wasn't the only one with doubts. Chavo was thinking of how Barkley had destroyed Hearns and Hearns had destroyed his dad, and he'd seen for himself how tall and strong Barkley was. He never told me this until later—didn't want to undermine my confidence.

Then a guy knocks on the door and says, "Durán, you're next." I was always moody and sullen before fights. This time, I was pissed off, too—but at the same time, completely relaxed, almost in a trance, as I kept repeating the same mantras:

Barkley does not belong in the same ring with me.
I am not washed up.
I am not the underdog.

"Why are you guys nervous?" I said to the room. "What's going on? Who's gonna die? Relax."

I was down to 156 pounds and I was confident as hell. That piece of shit wasn't going to beat me. I pissed a bunch of times on the dressing room carpet to lose a bit more. As usual, Plomo put some grease on my body that stank like hell, and when he'd finished, I started to shadowbox. Later de Cubas would say I got younger every minute the fight drew closer— he said I looked like the Durán who had fought against Davey Moore. "You are going to beat that son of a bitch, Durán!" he yelled.

Arum had put all the Olympians on the card that night, including Michael Carbajal, Anthony Hembrick, and the heavyweight Ray Mercer, as I recall. It was another sellout crowd at the Convention Center, with 7,500 fans screaming for the fight to start. Barkley had to lose a lot of weight, too, and looked lean and pumped. It was his first defense of the middleweight title. I got into the ring with de Cubas and Mike Acri and told them, *"Me voy a los palos con este negro."* I am going toe to toe with this black guy.

As soon as the bell rang, I got in a shot to the head with my right and then I backed off, cautious. I could have knocked him out within two or three rounds after hurting him like that, but I was a little afraid I was going to run out of air and

I needed to hold him at bay. "If I get tired," I thought, "this guy is going to come after me like a hurricane." So I changed the plan of attack. I never let his jab get to me and at the same time I eliminated his most powerful weapon, his right hand.

I went back to the corner after that first round and started thinking. In one minute, you have to think of everything. I told Plomo I was going to box him, not go for a quick knock-out, and that's what I did. He tried to jab me, but I kept blocking it and countered. I was more patient than I'd been in any other fight, spending the first six rounds just waiting for the right opportunity to launch into him. Meanwhile, he kept coming at me with some heavy body shots, but they didn't do any serious damage.

In the eighth round I got badly hit with a hook I didn't see coming. I was off balance, so he spun me around, which made it look much worse than it was. I came back to win the ninth and tenth rounds, hitting him with some bombs.

And then Barkley comes out hurt in the eleventh. Something must have happened that I hadn't clocked, because he was desperate. He was going to try to kill me or I was going to kill him and we were going at each other like crazy until the final minute of the round, when I caught him with a big right lead—*bam!* He was hurt. For good measure, I followed it up with a left-left-right combination—*boom!* With thirty seconds to go in the round, I kept coming hard at him, going for the kill. I hit him with an overhand right, a hook, a right to the ear, another hook, and a cross. *Buenas noches.* Good night. Barkley is down and everyone is going crazy.

But my wife doesn't know what's going on—once again, she's too scared to watch. She's on the phone to Panama, talking to her mother. "Mama, how's the fight going? Are they hitting him? Is he winning? Is he losing?"

"For God's sake, Fula, you're at the stadium—watch the fight!"

"Who's winning? Who's winning?"

"He knocked him down!"

"Who knocked who down? Is Roberto okay?"

"He knocked down Barkley!"

Joe Cortez, the referee, starts counting. "One, two, three . . ." Finally, Barkley is up at seven, but he's finished. He doesn't even know what corner he's supposed to go back to at the end of the round. What you don't see on the TV replay is that I saw him wobbling and jumped up in the air to hit him as hard as I could to make sure he went down. He managed to stay up in the twelfth, but I knew I had him. I bounced up and down, looking at him. He was beaten. What I told de Cubas was true: *Yo voy a descojonar este negro*. I'm going to tear this black guy's balls off.

I won a split decision, even though one of the judges, in-credibly, had Barkley winning, and there it was. I was a cham-pion again. *Un campeón*. Only the third fighter—and the first Latin—to capture major titles in four weight classes. *The Ring* magazine would name it "Fight of the Year." Everyone had seen it as a thirty-seven-year-old man fighting against a monster, but I remember a reporter asking me in the ring after the fight, "Roberto, your heart and determination is incredible. Where does it come from?"

"Panama City," I told him. "Republic of Panama. I love Panama. I love Miami. I love United States." When I was inspired by my country, you could not beat me. You had to kill me.

Donald Trump came into the dressing room and invited me to a post-fight party he was hosting, but I respectfully declined. When I came up to my hotel room, they filled the hot tub with ice and champagne, and the kids were carrying the championship belt around. I made $325,000 from that fight, and I deserved more, but right then it wasn't important: I was a world champion again—that was the only thing that mattered.

In Panama, people went crazy. There were firecrackers exploding across Panama City, and honking cars filled with people waving Panamanian flags, all heading to my house, where they lined up in front of the marble fountains, chanting my name. Someone told me the president had a plane waiting for me to go back to Panama. "No," I told them. "I'm going to Victor's Café. And then I'm going to Miami." I wanted this party to be the biggest and longest. I dedicated the fight to all the Cubans in Panama and Miami because the Panamanians had treated me so badly.

"You know, Durán, I love you and so do the Cuban people," Victor said to me in New York, "but remember you have your country."

"What am I going to do there?"

"If you want, I will go with you, Durán. I wish I had a country that was free I could go back to. Please promise me that when Cuba is free, you will come with me to Cuba."

"Of course."

A couple of days later we arrived back in Panama, while Victor stayed in New York. There were carnivals and parties all over the place, especially at my home. I was on top again, and all the *manzanillos* were tripping over one another trying to become my favorite. They would fight among themselves like scavengers to get closest to the pot of gold—plied me with everything they could think of, including women. They were brazen about it, too, showing up at our parties with whores. Fula obviously noticed, but they didn't seem to care. She'd throw whatever she could find at the *manzanillos*— glasses, plates, once even a great big chain—screaming, "Get those whores out of my house!"

Around that time, I took a party boat to Taboga, an island about twelve miles from Panama City, where I'd rented five rooms to hang out in and party. The boat accommodated only eight people, but we squeezed about twenty in—me, the *manzanillos*, women. Somehow, Fula got wind that I was with La China, my mistress at the time. So she decided to pay me a surprise visit. She told my kids and some cousins that they were going to the beach. The kids got all excited. But Fula had no intention of going to the beach. She was wearing a scarf, sunglasses, and a hat so people on the boat would not recognize her. When they got to the hotel, she told the kids to play with their Nintendos while she went downstairs for a moment.

Then she confronted me, La China, and the *manzanillos* in the bar. My mistress tried to leave, but Fula told her to sit down, staring at us, and made as if she had a gun in her purse—I'd given her a small pistol as a present not long before.

"Fula, don't do it!" I kept pleading.

"All it takes is one shot," she said. "One shot . . ."

Fortunately, nothing happened, and at the end of the day the *manzanillos* and my mistress had to go back to Panama City on the ferry. I went back on my boat with Fula and the kids as if nothing had happened.

That was our life. Complicated, as always. My wife tugging on one sleeve, the *manzanillos* on the other, and then there was the rest of my family . . .

One night, Pototo got into a fight, and I had to come to his rescue. Somebody had called the riot squad, and my brother and some other men were arrested for disorderly conduct. Fortunately for him, I got there before they took him to jail. As soon as the guards spotted me, they changed their tune, asking me for autographs and posing for pictures, but most important, the charges against Pototo were dropped.

But I still kept true to myself: beneath all the craziness that went on in my life since I'd become famous, I was really the same I always had been. I remember one particular day it was pouring down rain and I was wearing one of the expensive pairs of shoes I'd bought from Luis Gardini in New York all those years ago, which had cost me between $750 and

$900. I ran into an old friend of mine, a broadcaster for base-ball games, who stopped and stared at my shoes.

"Damn, Durán, those shoes are beautiful," he said. "You look sharp in those! Can I have them?"

"Take them," I said, and took them off.

"But it's raining."

"Doesn't matter." My socks got soaked, but I couldn't have cared less. I was probably happier to have gotten rid of them, and I went straight to a nightclub like that. I like to make people happy, and I'd rather have friends than enemies.

That includes my opponents. Men like the very first man to beat me, who came back into my life that year for unex-pected reasons. In April 1989, a friend got in touch: "Durán, I want you to go see Esteban de Jesús. He's dying of AIDS—he could go at any minute. It would mean a lot to him." I didn't hesitate, and along with Giovanni and Wiwa, I took my daughter Jovanna, who was fourteen.

De Jesús had gone downhill in a big way since we last fought in 1978. I heard he'd gotten very depressed after los-ing that fight and started smoking marijuana, snorting co-caine, and doing "speedballs" of cocaine and heroin. Then, in 1980, he shot someone in the head and was given a life sentence for first-degree murder. After his brother Enrique died of AIDS in 1985, Esteban tested positive, too; it turned out that the brothers had been sharing needles. The gover-nor of Puerto Rico had agreed he could be released to get treatment, and now he was in a hospital that was more like a drug treatment facility, in an abandoned milk factory in Río

Piedras. "I'm waiting to see what's to be God's will," I'd seen him saying in a TV interview. "I'm in God's hands."

When I set eyes on him, I felt so sorry for him. He was so skinny and frail and must have weighed less than a hundred pounds. The last time I'd seen him, he'd looked like a weight lifter—he'd been such a strong, muscular man. Now his speech was slurred, his eyes were watery, and he was out of it.

I leaned over to hug him but realized I might hurt him if I hugged him too tightly, so then I kissed him on the forehead. *"Tu siempre vas a ser mi campeón,"* I told him. You will always be my champion. José Torres, the former Puerto Rican fighter, was there, too, and took a picture of me hugging de Jesús that became quite famous. Jovanna was by the door, terrified at the thought of catching AIDS if she touched him. People didn't know as much about the disease back then. But I called her over and she hugged Esteban as well.

When he came around from the drugs he was on, we talked for a bit. He was barely conscious, but he knew who I was. And then we said good-bye, knowing we would never see each other again. Within a week, he was dead. He was thirty-seven—such a waste of a brilliant talent.

I earned a lot of respect for what I did, especially from the Puerto Ricans, even though that wasn't why I did it. I just wanted to be respectful and honor him, because we were no longer rivals, and I wanted him to die without pain. May he rest in peace.

NINE

"UNO MÁS"

I NEEDED TO MAKE PEACE AS WELL, but with myself. Leonard had yet to agree to take me on for the third time, which
was a fight I'd earned nine years before when I'd beaten the
odds and won the first encounter with him. What I didn't
find out until much later was that Leonard was still upset
about that fight, even though he'd beaten me since. He
couldn't handle it that everyone was still talking about me
and felt I hadn't paid him enough respect after he had beaten
me. I'd been waiting almost a decade: we were 1–1, and it was
logical to fight for a third time. But every time the subject
came up Leonard would say, "I want to fight you, but you
have to fight at 162 pounds."

"Why do I have to fight at 162 pounds if you are champion at 168?"

"I won't fight, then."

After I beat Barkley, de Cubas and Acri started negotiat-
ing with Bob Arum. They said they had a deal done with
Shelly Finkel, who was promoting Leonard, to fight him for

$12.5 million, but after Leonard and Hearns fought to a draw the deal blew up, because many people thought Leonard had lost. Now Arum offered me $7.5 million, which pissed me off: that third fight should have been my biggest payday. It was all a mess, and the delays only added to my feeling that Leonard was still afraid of me, particularly fighting at 168 pounds, which was now my normal fighting weight.

Chuleta. I was going to lose millions—a guaranteed purse of $7.5 million—if I didn't fight at the weight that suited Leonard. What made matters worse was that I'd just discovered I had a major problem with the IRS: an accounting error had meant I hadn't paid my taxes after the second fight with Leonard. I couldn't believe it. "I don't owe anyone anything," I said. I had trusted people to look after this shit for me; it wasn't my job to deal with the paperwork, it was my job to fight. I was being told only now, just when I'd spent pretty much all the money I had. Everyone was blaming everyone else and saying it was my fault that I didn't care enough about it. So I didn't have much choice. To pay my taxes, I had to fight Leonard at 162 pounds.

It got worse. Because I couldn't read English, I didn't know until after I'd signed the contract that it said that I'd forfeit $1 million for each pound I was overweight. Damn them! But in the end, I did make weight, and the guy who struggled was Leonard, who came in at 160 to my 158.

The date was to be December 7, 1989, at the Mirage in Las Vegas. Predictably, the slogan the promoters came up with was *"Uno más."*

So Leonard and I were to be rivals again, not only face-to-face in the ring but as adversaries from countries that didn't like each other. The run-up to the fight was not a good time for my country politically. The United States wanted to overthrow General Manuel Noriega, who'd already been indicted in the United States on drug trafficking charges. They were accusing him of suppressing democracy and endangering U.S. nationals, and to put pressure on him, they imposed economic sanctions. In October 1989, the United States supported a coup to try to oust him. It didn't work, but the Americans kept trying to squeeze him out and that made all of us Panamanians mad. People were looking for any excuse to get one over on America, and I didn't need a second invitation. "For Panama, I'm going to beat this loudmouth," I said in a TV advertisement that aired in my country. I also told them to be smart and bet on me.

By now, there wasn't the same hatred between me and Leonard there had been in the past; so much time had gone by, and so much had happened to both of us. We got along well—I was drinking champagne with him and his brother before the fight—but in public we had to keep up the rivalry because of the tension between our two countries.

Giant screens were being set up in the neighborhoods back home so the people of Panama could watch me fight. At the same time, the media was warning people to be on the alert, since this would be the best opportunity for another invasion by the U.S. forces. But many of the estimated 12,000 American soldiers stationed in Panama were going to be rooting for Leonard. There was a popular souvenir of a baseball cap with my name on it and four embroidered boxing titles. I told reporters I was going to add a fifth. For once, Fula decided she was going to be ringside, along with my mother—one of the rare occasions she left Panama to see me fight.

Of all the fights I have had in my career, this was the strangest. I felt exhausted before I even got in the ring. As I was leaving the dressing room, I said to de Cubas, "I can't feel my hands. They wrapped them too tightly." That was the first mistake my corner made. I also hadn't factored in the temperature: the cold was terrible that night—down in the forties—and I came into the ring in a silk robe. It looked great, with my name embroidered on the back, but I was freezing cold underneath, with the sweat coming off me from the warm-up in the dressing room. By contrast, Leonard came out in a full-length parka, and his corner put a blanket over him between rounds. In my corner, Carlos Hubbard and Plomo stuck to what we knew and put ice on me, as usual.

I didn't realize it until I was in the ring, but I could tell that my eyesight wasn't the same, that I couldn't see the punches coming; and while Leonard spent most of the night boxing and running, and I beat him up badly, I wasn't used to this feeling of not being able to see where the next punch was coming from. I had no regrets about my life out of the ring, but for the first time I could feel that my age had caught up with me. My legs were heavy, and no matter how much I tried, I couldn't dance.

In the end, I lost a unanimous decision, even though in the eleventh I had cut Leonard with a hard shot to his left eye that drew blood. Two of the judges scored it a ten-point margin for Leonard. The other scored it a five-point margin, which meant that Leonard retained his World Boxing Council middleweight title (160 pounds).

Afterward, Leonard was gracious, saying he was fighting a man who was thirty-eight years old. "He is a veteran, however, and he did come to fight." The punch stats said that he threw 150 fewer punches—438 to 588—but he connected on a lot more—227 to 84. Many of the 16,305 fans there that night were booing at the finish, and they didn't think it was a good fight. Neither did some of the writers. One of them called it a "slow, passionless waltz . . . Leonard's few flashes of brilliance were enough to earn a decision over Durán, who seemed almost indifferent." I was not indifferent. I just wasn't the same fighter; I didn't have that fire.

"He didn't win that fight," I said in the press conference. "Look at his face. He is going to remember me a long time." A lot of people agreed with me. "Blood leaked from a wide gash on his left eyelid," Pat Putnam wrote in *Sports Illustrated*. "Both lips were bloody from two cuts inside his mouth. More blood seeped from a cut on his right eyebrow. Except for the happiness spilling from his bright brown eyes, he had the look of a guy who had just been mugged in a saloon parking lot."

I had bigger problems to deal with that night. Whatever bullshit story I was given, I still don't know the truth about what happened. All I know is, at the end of the fight, for which my purse was $7.1 million, I got $2 to $3 million, and the rest went to the IRS. It was either that or go to prison. But now I was clear of the debt and could get on with the rest of my life.

That wasn't all. After the fight, the Tropicana Hotel, where we were staying, called de Cubas to say there was a problem: "A couple of guys were arrested, because there was blood in the bathtub. It looks like they killed somebody."

"No comas mierda," said de Cubas. That's bullshit. "That was from the chickens they killed for Santería to try and help Durán." It was a typical Santería tradition—offering a sacrifice to the gods in return for their help.

Back in Panama, my homecoming was pretty low-key, both because of the result of the fight and because people had more serious things on their minds, like whether we were going to get invaded. I got back in time for our daughter Jovanna's *quinceañera*—a tradition in Latin cultures of celebrating a girl's fifteenth birthday to signal her transition to adulthood. Jovanna's birthday was on December 10, but we celebrated it six days later. Fula prepared everything in Miami, including photos and centerpieces, as well as shoes and earrings for Jovanna and the dresses for the other girls, which Fula's aunt then altered. We brought in a chef from Miami, and he went to the Marriott Convention Center in Panama to prepare the food for eight hundred guests. I may have lost to Leonard, but I still knew how to have a good time! To this day, Jovanna's friends say it was the best *quinceañera* ever in Panama.

And then, on December 20, the United States invaded. I was in El Chorrillo at the time, in my car with about $3,000 on me, as I watched the American army trucks roll through, looking for General Noriega. But because I didn't pay much attention to the news, I hadn't heard we were being invaded, so I just kept driving to meet up with the friends I was going drinking with. When I got to the bar, it was empty. I went outside and there were all sorts of lights in the sky—blue, red, white. Everyone was screaming, "Invasion!"

The next day, we stayed together in front of the TV and watched the biggest disgrace in the history of our country, going on day and night. Hundreds of people were left dead, homes looted. Officials would later say 10,000 people were left homeless after the invasion, which ended with Noriega being captured and extradited to the United States. But for me the greatest sadness was what happened to my barrio in El Chorrillo. The area suffered a lot of damage. City blocks were burned down by the American troops to cut off possible escape routes for Panamanian soldiers.

But our problems were minor compared to many others'. A lot of Jovanna's friends had come over from the United States for her party, and now they couldn't leave. Stores were robbed and the streets turned into no-go areas. Even at home, we weren't untouched: we couldn't find a record of the money that Jovanna had been given as gifts, and it's likely some of it was stolen in the chaos.

With our TV and radio on all the time, I got more and more paranoid about what was going to happen to the country.

I got so worried about the financial situation that I went to the bank where I had all my money and took out $275,000. I put it in a suitcase to take to Miami. As soon as the travel restrictions were lifted, I checked the suitcase in at the airport, but when I landed in Miami it was gone. I never found it, and to this day, I don't know if one of the *manzanillos* had something to do with it or whether the airline made a mistake. I still had some money in the bank, though, and as soon as we could, we moved out of Panama and made our home in Miami. I took some more cash out, but this time I hid it under the bed for party money. The rest went pretty quickly on a new house and new car to give the kids some stability.

While I hadn't been around much for the kids, I had always been strict with them. Now that we were in Miami, I spent much more time with them, which allowed me to keep a closer eye on what they were up to and make sure they behaved themselves. "He's Chavo's friend," Jovanna and Irichelle would say when they were trying to sneak a boyfriend into the house, but I wasn't stupid. All I had to do was give them "the look"—the one I gave my opponents in the ring, which was pretty intimidating—and they knew they couldn't fool me.

By their second year in high school, the girls were asking to go to discos. "You have to be back in by one a.m.," I'd tell them. "One minute late and there'll be a problem." Sometimes they'd get back a little late, maybe one-fifteen, and they'd take their shoes off and try to sneak in quietly through the garage. But I'd be waiting for them, sitting inside, and I'd shine a flashlight on them: "When did I tell you to be back by? You're grounded for a month, and when you do go out again, I want you to call me every hour."

"Every hour?" they'd ask in horror.

"Yes."

I didn't mind them having boyfriends, but if those boys stepped out of line with my girls, I threatened to kill their entire families. I think they understood what I was saying; we didn't have a lot of problems after talks like that.

I'd tried to keep the girls in private school, but when the money got tight, we had to send them to public schools. We were still the Duráns, though, and people gawked and stared—who else had kids who showed up for school in a limo with a bar inside! The kids were so embarrassed, they used to ask our driver to drop them off in an alley near the school.

It was the same limousine I had to drive me to the night-clubs in Miami: I'd pick up my friends—I'd even go dressed in tennis shorts—and we'd fill the bar with whiskey and champagne and do the rounds of clubs, like Papa Grande on Coral Way and Douglas Road, Honey for the Bears on Southwest 27th Avenue, Mystique in Southwest Dade County, and the club at the Days Inn on Le Jeune. Although it was mostly about drinking and women, sometimes I'd get up on-stage and sing and play drums. At the end of the night we'd bring some girls back to the limo and I'd tell the doorman, "Don't let anyone near the car," and you can imagine what would happen next. It was one hell of a party. I was the king of Miami.

While things were still kicking off in Panama, more and more of my friends were moving to Miami, which meant I could revive the idea of the salsa band. I got a temporary group together—Los Tres Robertos, The Three Roberts—and we played some clubs in South Florida, including the Club Tropigala at the Fontainebleau Hotel. It was a fun way to make some money again. The other two Robertos—Roberto Ledesma and Roberto Torres—were international stars, Latin singers who had fans, records, and reputations. But audiences loved to see me, too—I'd go on last, with the band playing the theme from *Rocky* and four showgirls wearing big headdresses following me onstage. I'd wear a white robe, which I'd eventually take off, and I'd shout out to the crowd, "Let's go dancing!" as the music kicked in.

We'd kept on the house in Cangrejo, Panama, but it was getting harder to maintain both places, especially with Fula's brother always calling her to say he needed money for this and money for that. She'd send it to him, but it got to the point where we couldn't pay the bills, and it was no surprise when we lost the house in Miami and had to move to a hotel on 72nd Avenue until I could find somewhere for us to rent. It was the same old story: I was running short on cash but still insisted on showing people a good time. Fula was still going to the casinos. The spending had stayed the same, but our income was steadily decreasing. I knew of only one solution and that was to get back into action.

De Cubas and Acri finally set me up with a fight on the Mike Tyson–Razor Ruddock undercard at the Mirage against

Pat Lawlor. I was to be paid $250,000, and we set up camp at Caron's gym. One day, de Cubas said, "Let's go see Mickey Rourke." I knew him as the actor who thought he was a boxer; now Rourke had split up from his wife and was sleeping at the gym, and of course he wanted to spar against me. I didn't warm up properly and messed up my left shoulder sparring with him. But I also picked up this strange fever I couldn't shake off. I thought they were going to suspend the fight, but it turned out I wasn't the only one with money problems: one of my handlers was in the shit as well—he'd signed off on a dry-cleaning business in New York and had bought somewhere between ten and fifteen laundry machines he was going to have to pay for after the fight. "You've got to fight," he told me. "I'm not going to lose that money." Part of me couldn't believe this was what my boxing career had come to: getting into the ring to pay for some dry-cleaning machines.

Pat Lawlor should have been an easy fight—I was an eight-to-one favorite—but I went into it with a fever and my left shoulder was shot, which meant I had to abandon my fight plan, and I lost by TKO in the sixth round when I couldn't continue. The doctor said I also tore my biceps near my left shoulder. Even though I had only one arm, I thought I could still fight. Some boxing people called it another *No más*, but that was bullshit. Lawlor didn't beat me at my best. I vowed everyone would see what happened when I was healthy and fought him in Panama.

It took a while for the injury to my left shoulder—my rotator cuff—to heal, so I wasn't able to fight for eighteen months.

Eventually, de Cubas and Acri got me involved with promotions for USA Network, which was starting to carry fights on Tuesday nights, many staged at the casino in Bay City, Mississippi. I wasn't getting a lot—between $50,000 and $75,000, minus expenses and manager's fees—but I did three fights there, starting with Jacques LeBlanc in June 1993, which took me into my third decade in the boxing ring.

American boxing writers were no longer calling me Hands of Stone: they were mocking me now, calling me "Belly of Jelly." That might have been started by LeBlanc himself as part of the pre-match promotion, but he was too much of a coward to admit it. "He has little respect for the master," I said. "Since he's been saying things, he's going to pay." I was in good shape for that fight and won by a unanimous ten-round decision.

I had a good time there with all those cowboys and rednecks. The fights would sell out every time, with about 5,000 people at the arena, and I used to ham it up for them by wearing a Confederate flag into the ring. But I wasn't happy about the money—one night, as they were paying the fighters in the casino office, I remember shouting, *"Ladrones!"*— Thieves!—at de Cubas and Acri, but we always worked it out in the end.

They were trying to bring me back and get me paid big money again, but they didn't want to take any risks, so they were picking opponents for me who just stood in front of me, guys I couldn't miss. During that time, I may not have been in the top four or five in my weight class, but I was still competitive enough, and I could still fight, even though I knew I was now on the way down and the days of being able to bust my ass to make weight in a championship fight were over.

On December 14, 1993, I fought Tony Menefee in what would be the hundredth fight of my career. At forty-two, I was fighting a guy half my age, who was mostly a club fighter who made a couple of hundred dollars when he fought. I was old enough to be his father and that was pretty depressing. Even I hadn't thought I would be boxing at this age.

I almost pulled out because I didn't feel good, and delayed leaving for Mississippi until two weeks before the fight, which meant the change of weather hurt me. I caught a cold and had a temperature of 102 the day before, but I decided to fight since the people at Casino Magic and in Mississippi had been good to me. Besides, it had already been pushed from November to December because I'd had a knuckle injury, so it would have been very difficult to reschedule.

Menefee thought he could beat me because I was old, but what I'd lost in speed I made up for in experience, and there was no way his style of run-and-clutch was going to work on me. By the time we touched gloves, I could see he was afraid of this old man. What he hadn't realized until too late was that people like me who had nothing to lose, who just wanted to survive, were the hardest to beat. After what I'd been through, I'd rather die in the ring than get beat. And you don't know what that experience is until you've been there yourself. No one can teach it to you, you can't train for it, but after your fists, it's your most powerful weapon in the ring.

I won by TKO in the eighth round. I'd hurt him with two rights, and then I gave him another flurry and he had to take a standing eight count. I was the one who stopped the fight, basically: I didn't want to hurt the guy any more—he was a young fighter—so I looked at the referee. The fans booed, but it was the right decision. "If I hadn't stopped, I would have killed him," I said afterward. It was my ninety-first victory and my sixty-third knockout. I told people I felt like a young kid again.

IN 1993, it was finally safe to return to Panama—though it took years for the country to recover fully from the mess the U.S. invasion left behind—so we went back to Cangrejo. It was supposed to be a nice homecoming, but it turned into a nightmare. The house was deserted and empty. My brother-in-law, who'd been staying there while we were in Miami, had sold everything. The bills hadn't been paid, there was no furniture, no electricity, and no water. He'd been using the money I sent him—money that was supposed to help take care of things in Panama—to gamble, and the minute he heard we were on our way back, he disappeared. It turned out he'd even sold off my championship belts and my guns. I was in such a rage over what he'd done that my kids were scared I was going to kill him. I managed to control my emotions in front of them, but I wanted revenge. All we could do, however, was file a police report and in the meantime try to get our lives back together. The kids had to take showers at their friends' houses, since we didn't have hot water for months. We were a proud family and we tried to keep all of this to ourselves, but they were really hard times.

I began to think about doing things outside boxing. I announced I was going to run for the Senate in Panama—it was my mother's idea, a way of getting me out of the ring once and for all. I knew the people, she kept telling me; I knew what it was like to be poor, and the people needed someone like me. I shouldn't have listened to her or let my friends talk me into running. But I'd made a promise to my mother and I wouldn't break my word. So I decided to run in the May 1994 election to represent El Chorrillo.

I also made a promise to myself: I vowed to win my sixth world title. After beating Menefee, I signed up for my first fight in Europe, in the South of France, against Carlos Montero in Marseille.

I was busier than ever, going back and forth between Miami and Panama, as I tried to get my political career going. My daughter Jovanna had wanted to go back to Miami because she'd had a boyfriend in high school there; somehow, we managed to scrape enough money together to rent an apartment in Miami Lakes and she stayed there with me.

We set up camp at the DiLido Hotel in Miami Beach. I liked to go running along the beach, and one day this guy came up to me, yelling, "Give me your money! Give me your money!"

"I haven't got any money."

He came after me and threw sand in my eyes. I covered

up, waited for him to get close, and—*bam!*—I dropped him. But when I hit him, the callus I had on my right hand from training opened up and started bleeding. The guy must have been on drugs, because he got up right away as if he wasn't hurt. *Chucha la madre!* "You want to box?" he's screaming. "You want to box?" He starts moving like he's shadowboxing. So I hit him again. He goes down. He throws sand in my eyes again—*bam!* I ran back to the hotel and stayed in my room. I could see from my window he was coming back with a bunch of guys.

In France I found a doctor to sew up my hand so I was able to fight, and I beat Montero in a ten-round decision for my sixth consecutive victory. Then I made it seven in a row by beating Terry Thomas back at Casino Magic in March 1994. I was climbing the mountain again.

TEN

PAZ
AND
MACHO
TIME

THE LEGEND VERSUS THE COMEBACK KID, they were calling it. I was going to fight Vinny Pazienza in Atlantic City for the International Boxing Council super-middleweight title on June 25, 1994, at the Las Vegas MGM Grand. It was a good payday, too: $500,000.

Pazienza had disrespected me, calling me ugly, no better than a dog. "He can't speak good English," he said at a press conference, "but I bet you he can box like a German shepherd." He threatened de Cubas. He disrespected my country and called me a coward and a quitter. "Who else has he fought besides Leonard?" he asked the reporters. "Guys like Kirkland Laing. Please." My team thought he was juiced up. He certainly looked all bloated, and he hung out with muscleheads. I just smiled and reminded reporters that in 1991 he'd broken his neck in a car accident: "I'm going to break his neck again."

I'd lost a month of training while I'd been running for

the Senate. It's true what people say—politics is dirtier than boxing. I thought I could go into politics without getting sucked into the corruption we'd seen in Panama for years. I lost the election, and vowed never to waste that time again.

But I felt good. I entered the ring wearing a baseball cap with TEACHER on it: I was going to give this guy a lesson. I was coming in as a former champion, with 564 rounds of professional ring experience; he was just a punk. The lesson started when I knocked him down at the end of the second round, but the referee called it a slip. In the third I cut him on the lip, and then in the fifth I dropped him with a right hand. By the end of the fight he was bleeding all over his forehead and looked like a complete mess.

We knew he was going to use the Reyes gloves, which have high ridges on them, to rake across my face, but all he managed to do was slap me with a couple of wild shots. It helped that we'd asked for an eighteen-foot ring to keep him from running so I could work him over properly. He kept hitting me after the bell, talking trash, cheap-shot bullshit. He stuck his tongue out at me like a baby, and held the rope with one of his hands, but I ignored all his nonsense.

I thought I'd outpunched him, and at the end of the twelfth round my corner picked me up and lifted me onto their shoulders. When the ring announcer called Pazienza the winner, I threw my hands up in disgust. "If this kid is so tough," I said afterward, "look at his face and look at mine. What did he do? He slapped the whole night. I didn't lose the fight. The decision really made me mad, and I'm going to make this kid pay."

After the fight, I sat down at a table with Tommy Brunette, a boxing promoter from Minnesota who'd been in the business for years, and we played dominoes for a long time and drank beer. By the time we were done, we'd gotten through two and a half cases.

I didn't have to wait long to get even with Pazienza. In October, I beat Heath Todd, and then the rematch was scheduled for Atlantic City in January 1995. Another good purse: $615,000.

Before the second Pazienza fight, Charlie Sheen came to visit me—there were still a lot of Hollywood stars interested in a boxing legend like me. Once, I'd enjoyed the distractions all these actors and actresses brought, but now I wasn't in the mood. Vinny Pazienza was still a clown and a bigmouth, and I wanted to shut him up. "Last time, I beat him up," I told reporters, "but this time I'm going to put him in the hospital . . . They're going to have to put a big Band-Aid on his face."

I wanted to beat the crap out of him even more after he disrespected my son Victor, who was only three then. He called him a "stupid little kid," though later he tried to change it to "lovable, stupid little kid." You don't talk that way about a three-year-old child. That made me want to destroy him even more.

It was a tougher fight than the first one. I was more sluggish, and one of the announcers called me "Feet of Stone." With about twenty seconds to go, Pazienza pulled a cartilage in his rib throwing a punch, but it was too late. He won by unanimous decision. But I was still standing at the end, even though Pazienza said he hit me with some shots that would have knocked a wall down.

He also said I should take up golf, which made me mad because it showed he still had no respect for me. But I had no intention of retiring and that year I fought twice more, both TKO victories. I knocked out Roni Martinez in Kansas City as part of the card featuring Tommy Morrison and Razor Ruddock. Then I fought in South Florida, at the Fort Lauderdale Memorial, and knocked out Wilbur Garst in four rounds. Santiago Samaniego, my cousin, who was a junior middleweight, fought on that card, too. He went on to become a world champion.

I still had dreams of winning that sixth world title, but it was getting difficult both to make weight and have the will-power to keep training. Even though I knew I was making life harder for myself, I couldn't help it, and I'd be up to my usual tricks of hiding stuff under the bed: Coke, Nestlé's Crunch bars—and all the rest of the stuff every trainer I've had has tried to keep away from me. And the older I got, the harder it was to take the pounds off. But those were my habits, and there was no way I could change. I'd be trying to make weight at 165, and two weeks before a fight everybody'd think we were good because I was at 172. But then I'd step on the scale and I'd weigh 175. Plomo and my son Robin, who was now part of my team, would get very suspicious. "What happened? The scale must be wrong."

No, the scale wasn't wrong. Plomo and Robin just couldn't babysit me twenty-four hours a day. I was a great boxer, but I was also very good at sneaking stuff I wanted and hiding it away. I couldn't help myself. Sometimes I'd get up in the middle of the night, open the fridge, and eat everything in it.

Eventually, I'd bust my ass to make weight, but I was so dehydrated, I had to build my strength back up: two liters of Coca-Cola, five bottles of Gatorade. Robin would tell me I needed to go easy, but I wouldn't listen. Coffee, Coke, milk shakes, spaghetti, steaks—sometimes I'd get so full, I'd throw up. Before one of those fights in South Florida, I even started puking on my way to the ring.

At least there was some good news around that time. In November 1995, I finally got my five world championship boxing belts back. They'd been recovered in Miami by FBI agents—a guy by the name of Luis Báez had gotten them from my brother-in-law and had been trying to sell them to a sports memorabilia shop in New York for $200,000. Fortunately for me, the store owner was cooperating with the FBI in another investigation, and I got the tip-off. Báez claimed I'd handed them over to him because I owed him money.

My brother-in-law did do some time in jail for it, but the law in Panama says relatives can't press charges against one another, so he was let go after a while. Fula accepted all the blame—she knew I might have killed him. But look what he'd done to me and my family.

. . .

When I beat Ray Domenge by a unanimous decision in Miami in February 1996, it was my third consecutive win after losing for the second time to Pazienza. And now I was back to where I wanted to be, chasing another championship. This time, it was Héctor "Macho" Camacho in Atlantic City in June 1996 for the vacant IBC middleweight title. The IBC was a relatively new sanctioning body, established in 1990, outside of the "Big Four" that had dominated boxing rankings. The fight was called "Legend to Legend: Camacho vs. Durán," on a card that also featured Buster Douglas, who'd recently caused a massive upset by beating Tyson in Japan. I was forty-five, but so what? I was passing all the tests: not only did I have the body of a young man, but as one of the doctors told me before the fight, I also had a very thick skull, so there was no way he could stop me from fighting.

Camacho tried to psyche me out while we were promoting the fight, sending me videotapes of him telling me I'd never be like Muhammad Ali, never be like Sugar Ray Leonard, and of course talking nonsense about the Macho Man. "I'm playing with his head," Camacho told people. "He's going to lose the same way I lost to Julio César Chávez, like a champion. But the bottom line is that reality is going to smack him in the face."

I laughed. What else could I do? Why should I give a shit about a guy who loves to dance in the ring, talking crap about me? I told him I hoped he didn't sing when we fought. He sucked at singing.

During fight week Camacho actually told a reporter from *The New York Times* that he'd cried because I made fun of him. He'd grown up with me as his idol: "I was hurt by the way he was acting. He knows I'm a straight-up guy. I'll clown around with my friends. But I tried to be tactful with him, and instead, he started going after me. When my adrenaline gets that high, I'm used to unleashing it." He never wanted to be mean like me, he said. Maybe he should have taken ballet lessons.

We fought at 160 pounds. In a poll of twenty-two boxing writers before the fight, nineteen had Camacho winning. But I had a good camp and came to Atlantic City three days before, feeling great and weighing 157. De Cubas was so confident that he actually bet $5,000 on me—the only fight he ever bet on in his life. I was a seven-to-one underdog.

And so we fought. Camacho didn't look like a ballerina the night we fought, but he did come in wearing some ridiculous Egyptian outfit. Who did he think he was, King Tut? I'd gotten a buzz cut at the barbers to show people that even though I was forty-five, I was serious about this shit. After the referee had given us our instructions, Camacho wouldn't touch gloves. I was ready to go.

Right away Camacho began playing patty-cake with his jab while I was killing him with body shots. *Boom! Boom! Boom!* Most of his jabs never landed, but I could sense those body shots were doing damage. So was my right-hand lead.

After the fifth round, I picked up strength and became the only man in the ring. I thought I'd won at least seven of the twelve rounds. He never hurt me, and all I could see were the welts all over his face and body.

At the end we hugged, out of respect. Our cornermen lifted us both in the air to celebrate victory. I was sure I'd won. And then they read out the results cards from the judges.

It was a unanimous decision: 115–113, 116–113, 117–111.

De Cubas was pissed off, maybe because he lost all that money. As the announcer was interviewing Camacho he shouted, *"Durán ganó esa pelea!"* Durán won that fight! Even Leonard called it a horrible decision, and "an early Christmas gift" for Camacho. The announcer said I was tarnishing my memories and legacy by continuing to fight. What was that all about when I was in such good shape? And who was he to lay down the law on what I did for a living?

I fight. End of story.

I HAD TWO MORE FIGHTS that year, both victories. Only one was in the United States—a sixth-round TKO of Mike Culbert in Chester, West Virginia. I began 1997 in a bad way, losing to Jorge Castro by a unanimous decision in Argentina. Four months later, however, I was able to avenge that loss in spectacular fashion—my hundredth career victory. Better yet, it was on the eve of my forty-sixth birthday and I was fighting in front of my people in Panama. I nearly knocked Castro out in the third round but won a close ten-round decision. All three judges scored it 97–95. The crowd—about 10,000—went crazy, but I could hardly celebrate. I was so exhausted, I couldn't even comment to reporters after the bout. Then, in November, I traveled to South Africa to fight Britain's David Radford.

Four days before the fight, the promoter comes into the gym and says, "Stop training. Nelson Mandela wants to meet you. I've brought Leonard here—and a lot of other fighters," he went on, "and Mandela's never wanted to meet them. But when he found out *you* were here . . ."

We went to the presidential home in Pretoria, and I was greeted by two women in long flowing dresses. When Mandela set eyes on me, he exclaimed, "Stone Hands!" He was already seventy-nine and had been in prison for twenty-seven years. He was happy as hell. Marvin Hagler was there, too, as part of the promotion. We walked across the lawn, and Mandela put his arms around both of us. "They have put boxing on a new footing," he said, "because the days of shuffling and slogging it out are past. These are days when you know to quote Muhammad Ali: 'A boxer floats like a butterfly and stings like a bee.'" Then we all walked back to the house.

I held Mandela's arm as we went up the steps, and he started telling me his life story, with a friend of mine translating. Before being imprisoned, Mandela had been an amateur boxer, and he was still a big boxing fan, even though he'd been locked up during my whole career.

When reporters asked me what I'd felt on meeting Mandela, all I could say was that he was a great president. "He's known all over the world, and especially in Panama. It's a great honor for me today."

I went on to beat Radford, and then Félix José Hernández in January 1998, but they were *muertos*, dead guys. I still wanted the big fight, but my promoters were telling me they couldn't do it. I didn't see why not. I even went to some restaurants in Los Angeles where I knew Julio César Chávez liked to go, to see if we could make it happen. I never found him. I heard he didn't want to go past 150 pounds—I was pretty sure that was just an excuse. The Mexican was a good boxer, and I respected him and all that, but he wasn't born in the era of Roberto Durán. Chávez would never, ever have beaten me. Poor guy—he would not have lasted three rounds.

So Chávez was out but William Joppy was in. Don King gave me that opportunity—to fight Joppy in August 1998 for the WBA middleweight title.

De Cubas went crazy when I told him. He was after a rematch with Camacho because he wanted me to fight slower, older guys—guys who were beatable. "Why would you want William Joppy?" he said. "He's a full-fledged middleweight. Why would Don King put you, at forty-seven, against somebody in his prime when I've spent my whole time protecting you from fighters who are twenty years younger?" He wasn't the only one to point out that when I fought Benny Huertas in 1971, Joppy was two days short of his first birthday. De Cubas said he'd have nothing to do with it and didn't want to work with me anymore.

The reason I took the fight? Money—plain and simple.

Good money, too: $250,000. I wouldn't see any of it, though: what wasn't going to the IRS to cover more back taxes I owed was going to pay child support in Miami. The IRS agent even had the balls to come and sit at ringside to wait for his money.

I just wanted to win; I could worry about making more money later. It was my twenty-fifth appearance in a world title fight. "I've been taking care of myself," I thought. "I'll knock him out."

The fight was originally scheduled for June 6, 1998, on the undercard of Evander Holyfield–Henry Akinwande at Madison Square Garden—King had put us on it because my name would sell a lot more tickets than the other guys. But Akinwande tested positive for hepatitis B, so the date was changed to August 28, at the Hilton in Las Vegas. *Chuleta!* I wasn't pleased. I loved fighting in New York at the Garden: I'd fought seven times there in my career and lost only once— to de Jesús in 1972. But at least in Vegas there were a couple of thousand fans there—a sellout for that place—and lots were there to see me win.

The ringside announcer kicked things off by saying I wasn't Stone Hands anymore, I was powder-puff hands. In the second round Joppy started getting in some good upper-cuts, but I managed to tag him with a hard right-hand lead to start the third. He recovered quickly, though, and got me with a right at the end of the round that sent me reeling against the ropes. He kept coming after me, hitting me with more shots to the face and body. He tried to get me down, but I wouldn't go. Still, he kept chopping away at me until finally the referee, Joe Cortez, stopped the fight. There were six seconds left in the round, and I was trying to tell him I was okay—no problem.

Cortez said he'd given me every chance, but from the first round it was just a matter of time. His job's to protect the fighter, and he stopped the fight when he saw I'd taken one punch too many.

Joppy was respectful after beating me. He told reporters I was a great man, and how he'd grown up watching me and admiring me. He loved me, he said. But he also said that now he was the man. It was a bad night for me. There were all the old problems, but I also knew that my eyesight wasn't what it had been. I confided in Tony Gonzalez, the guy who was now managing me who was also my daughter Irichelle's husband, and he took me to a doctor. It was clear I couldn't see properly, but he didn't want to operate.

De Cubas said he cried that night, and called Don King one of the biggest sons of bitches he'd ever come across for letting me fight Joppy.

So my losing streak in Vegas continued. Since beating Luigi Minchillo in 1989, I hadn't won a single fight there: Benítez, Hagler, Hearns, Sims, Leonard, Lawlor, Pazienza—and now Joppy.

Now everyone really thought I was finished.

ELEVEN

ONE
MORE
FOR
LA PATRIA

I WAS NOW FIGHTING in my fifth decade as a professional boxer. Who the hell does that? Apart from the great Jack Johnson, no one in boxing history except me. I was forty-eight years old, with so many fights, and so many memories since that *pelao* had made his professional debut in 1968 in Colón as a lightweight. Now I was old and fat and, yes, had seen better days, but I still wanted one last hurrah.

The promoter called it "The Battle of Five Decades" and it was for the NBA super-middleweight title, in June 2000, against Pat Lawlor. Okay, a lot of people didn't think that it was in the same league as the WBA or WBC championship, but it was a world title, and that's what the record books will say.

And it was in Panama. It had been a couple of years since I'd fought there, and the most important thing for me was for the Panamanian people to enjoy this fight. I promised them I'd make Lawlor pay for that TKO in 1991. I had never lost in Panama. I wasn't going to start now.

In my prime, I'd had that huge entourage—all those *manzanillos*: a guy to carry my gloves, another guy for my bag, a guy to do the laundry, a guy to do the cooking . . . That was all gone. Plomo was the only one from El Chorrillo in the 1960s who'd stayed loyal all these years; otherwise, it was just Tony Gonzalez and my son Robin. Robin did the dishes, the cleaning, and the cooking. He took care of my laundry, all the interpreting, and everything else I needed to get in shape for a fight. He'd be up at five-thirty to get me ready to go running—he'd even come out with me—and when we got back, he'd get breakfast ready.

Plomo drew up a daily schedule of road and bag work, and then we'd finish with eight rounds of sparring. He was tough on this old man! The gym was located in San Miguelito, in Panama City, and it was hot and shabby, just like in the old days. But I wasn't a kid anymore: I knew that. Two weeks before the fight, I was already down to the 168-pound limit.

The fight was at the arena that had been named after me, and on that night it was packed. They brought me in on a crane, and as I looked down on the crowd I could see all my family—my wife, my sons, my daughters, cousins, friends . . . It felt like I was flying.

And then, as the dry ice was turned on, they played "Patria," the famous Rubén Blades song. *"Patria son tantas cosas bellas,"* it reminds us, *"patria* is so many beautiful things." As the song says, our homeland is everything in the soul of our people and the cries of our martyrs; it is not the "lessons of dictatorships or imprisonments" or oppression.

For Panamanians, this song touches the heart: it stands for so much, especially after all the shit we'd been through in the last few years. As I looked down I could see sons and fathers and grandsons hugging one another—all the generations here together, crying and celebrating my name and my legacy. That's what boxing means to these people: it's powerful enough to bring everyone in the nation together even when everything else in their lives is falling apart.

I beat Lawlor by a unanimous twelve-round decision and I was a world champion again. I had done it—on my forty-ninth birthday, in my own country, and with all my people around me. It was a magical moment.

There was so much emotion among the people in the arena—such a release—that things got out of hand. The chaos got so bad, the police had to come and fire tear gas to control the crowd. It didn't faze me, but it wasn't what I wanted at all to mark such a special victory.

Afterward, Robin went off to college in Miami, before coming back to study in Panama. He did everything his way—independently. I had no idea at the time, but to pay for his tuition he did the shittiest jobs going. It was only years later that he told me he didn't want to be a twenty-one-year-old kid asking his father for money to go out with a girl. He didn't want to live off the Durán name. He still gets pissed off when people say my family takes advantage of my name.

They don't know us. Yes, having a last name like Durán helps you a lot, don't get me wrong. But all it does is open a door; it's up to you to keep it open and walk through. If you suck at your job, they're going to fire your ass—doesn't matter if you're a Durán or not.

Now that the kids were grown up, it wasn't just my cornermen who asked why I kept on fighting, even though I was nearly fifty. "Why's your dad fighting again?" Robin's friends would ask him. He'd ask me himself: "Why? *Why?* Why are you doing it again?"

"I've got to," I told him. "I'm not done. I can beat all these kids."

Fula never asked me to stop fighting, even though as I came to the end of my career and she saw how much I was struggling to make weight, she got more and more scared. She knew that whatever she said, I was going to keep fighting, whether she liked it or not, and that I needed her to support me. She understood—she always has. Even when I was suffering and sweating, this was my life and my choice. My legacy wouldn't be damaged if I lost a few fights when I was past my prime. All those *pelaos* who fought me wished they had half the career I'd had, and a fraction of the titles, and when they stepped into the ring with me, they were nervous and respectful. They were fighting Roberto Durán, and there was only one fighter who could beat Durán and that was Durán himself.

A friend of mine, Félix Piñango, once compared me to Barabbas the gladiator: a man who's earned his freedom from the ring and been offered all the good things in life but spurns them. He wants to die in the arena. That, said Félix, was me.

No, it isn't. I never wanted to die in the ring. But why wouldn't I want wealth and luxury? Why the hell not? Yes, I fought for pride, and because I thought no man could ever beat me, but I loved the money. I gave it away because I never forgot that I was a *pelao* from El Chorrillo and that there are many, many people from El Chorrillo who never made a tiny bit of the money I made.

But there has to be an end: it happens to all the great fighters. For me, it finally came on July 14, 2001, when I fought Héctor Camacho again, this time in defense of my NBA super-middleweight title. I didn't know it would be my last fight, but I did know that Plomo and I were nearing the end of the road. We spent the time away from the gym doing what we had done since I was a *pelao*—playing dominoes, playing chess. "We started this together," I told him, "and we're finishing it together."

The fight with Camacho was going to be in Denver, Colorado, and we went to South Beach, Florida, for our training camp. I was happy to have Robin back and by my side, although he was doing his schoolwork at the same time. He wasn't sleeping well, had no life of his own, but I could see he was happy taking care of me. He was doing a good thing for his father.

Robin told me that we should be going to Denver at least a month before the fight so I could get acclimatized to the altitude there. "He's not thirty anymore," he said to Tony Gonzalez. "He's not even thirty-five. He's fifty. It's not the same."

"No," said Gonzalez. "Two weeks'll be plenty."

The first day in training camp I was flying. I was knocking out sparring partners, I was putting in excellent roadwork, an hour or an hour and a half at a time, which would have been good going for a fighter half my age.

But that was before we got to Denver. I had never felt that kind of altitude. I was sucking air from the first day I got there. In the first training session I got on the treadmill and before I knew it I felt like I was suffocating.

"Dude, you've only been running twenty-five minutes," Robin told me.

"I can't breathe."

That brought the morale down. I'd get tired just going for a walk. When I sparred, it felt like I was getting hit by a heavyweight. I should have listened to Robin, because if I'd known this was how I was going to feel, I would have gone to Denver much earlier.

They promoted the fight as "When Legends Collide." The American press had a lot of fun with that. One guy called it "When Legends Collapse," because our combined age was eighty-nine.

Of course Camacho and I still loved to talk shit to each other—what do you expect? I was Panamanian, he was Puerto Rican, we weren't going to shake hands and play chess. I was going to try to kick his ass and he was going to try to kick mine. He said I was too old and shouldn't believe in miracles, that I was going to try to do the impossible, and he was ready for the impossible, and that if he lost to me, he was going to retire. I told him he was a clown: Camacho the clown. He'd look good, I thought to myself, if he walked into the ring wearing one of those big red noses.

I felt I could still compete, but on that night Camacho had a pretty good right jab and left hook. Before the start of the twelfth, as my cornermen were yelling, "Three more minutes!" the referee, Robert Ferrara, came to my corner and told me, "You're still the greatest." I went out and fought, and now my corner was screaming, *"Tu primero, Cholo, tu primero!"* You first, Cholo, you first! But I had no gas left. Still, Camacho couldn't knock me out! That shows you how tough I was.

I lost a unanimous twelve-round decision, but I felt that I had won that fight. And that was the last time, it turned out, that I stepped into the ring. A few months later I was in the car accident.

On January 26, 2002, I called a press conference to announce my retirement. I really had no choice. My rehabilitation was going to take too long, and the doctors had already told me to give up. "Boxing is my life," I said. "But right now I don't want to think about it. I am still exercising," I told the press, "so that when all the honors arrive, people will see me in good shape." I'd come out of the hospital just as Diego Maradona's farewell match was taking place: "I don't want to look all fat like Maradona," I added. There was going to be a lot to celebrate: all the world titles, 103 victories. Apart from 1985 and 1990, I had fought at least once every single year since 1968.

And that was the end of the road for Durán the boxer. I guess if it hadn't been for the accident, I would have kept on fighting, even though I was fifty, until there was absolutely no one left to fight. It was still a thrill for people to see Roberto Durán, the legend, in action. But I also think I loved to fight so much that if I had kept fighting, I might've died in the ring. Not because someone was hitting me and hurting me, but because of what I was putting my body through to get in shape to fight. I think God wanted me to retire not as punishment but as prevention, so I'd still be alive today. I suspect my family wanted me to retire, too, even though they respected my wishes.

After I retired, two of my children, Chavo and Irichelle, went into boxing. I wasn't a big fan of the idea, but their mother was, and they knew it was going to piss me off if they tried to keep it a secret. I didn't even want to see them fight. It was one of the reasons I got into boxing—so my children wouldn't have to. I don't think my other children were in favor, either: it was worse for them seeing Chavo and Irichelle fight.

Irichelle, who lived with her mother in Miami, got interested because Muhammad Ali's daughter started fighting. Irichelle fought three times between 2000 and 2002, in New Orleans, Panama City, and Las Vegas. She trained for seven months in Australia, and even had Chavo come out and help her train for her first fight, in Vegas. She lost a four-round split decision, and said she was overwhelmed by the crowd and the media.

Irichelle fought twice more, winning once and losing once. I was so disgusted that for a while I didn't even talk to her. Why? Because when I fought, I knew what I was doing. My children didn't have all that experience and ring craft. And Irichelle was very feminine; she was not a typical female boxer. Jovanna went to the fight in New Orleans, and she heard some of the fans whistling at Irichelle and calling her a "sexy bitch." Some boxing writers called her "Little Miss Hands of Stone." Irichelle didn't need that kind of nonsense in her life.

My son Chavo was good, even though he didn't have any amateur experience. He started fighting at twenty-seven and won five fights between 2000 and 2004, with two knockouts. He lost one fight, and one was a no-decision. I saw him fight twice, once in Argentina and once in Panama City. Julio César Chávez's son was coming up then, too. Chavo would have beaten the crap out of him, because Chavo was tall and had a great understanding of boxing—he knew how to block punches and he knew how to hit. Perhaps he could have become a world champion, but I got him out of boxing. A fan once came up to him at one of his fights and said, "I didn't come to see you fight. I just came to see if your father was here. Don't bring shame on your father's name—go out and win."

I knew it had to be tough for my children because of my

name and my legacy, but I'd rather they didn't fight at all. I was once asked how I felt when I saw them fighting. "I don't feel anything," I said. "I know my little animals. Boxing is not for them." But they were competitive, just like me. I didn't like to lose at anything—billiards, softball, whatever. I always took the contest to another level, and I passed that competitiveness on to my children.

In 2005, I reconnected with Mike Tyson. He was at the end of his career and having a lot of problems. He'd filed for bankruptcy in 2003, and he was pretty much finished in the ring, losing to a nobody called Danny Williams in the summer of 2004. He was out of money and still doing drugs, and had lost his entourage now that he had no money; when he fought Williams, his security guy had worked his corner. Williams knocked Tyson out in the fourth round, down and out against the ropes. Tyson was thirty-eight now; he'd injured his knee in the fight with Williams and he needed surgery.

I'd always liked him, and I understood that boxing's always going to be a struggle when you get older. Tyson was on the last run, but he was going to give it one last shot against a fighter named Kevin McBride, and the plan was for me to work with him. He was training in California with de Cubas, who'd set up a camp at Paso Robles, up in the hills, and had brought in Buddy McGirt, who at the time trained Antonio Tarver and Arturo Gatti. We all met up in Los Angeles and drove up to see Tyson. It was a pain in the ass to get there— three hours from Los Angeles, maybe more, up hills and down, up and down—to this big complex with two houses and a gym downstairs, everything spread out over 159 acres. The owners were from Germany—de Cubas said they owned Porsche.

Now here we were, two badasses who were no longer in their prime but who respected each other. Fans loved us or hated us, but they respected us, too. It wasn't a Panamanian thing or an American thing, it was a boxing thing, and at our peak, we were the best and the baddest at it.

Tyson didn't have much left, obviously, but at least we had a good time messing with his head. He was terrified of the huge tarantulas out in the compound. There was a cemetery near the house that had six Germans buried in it, and we would tell Tyson that the German ghosts would come out at night, looking for him. I got de Cubas to tell him that at night the Martians would come down to take the black people away. "Look, Tyson—up in the sky—it's a UFO coming to get you!"

"Fuck you, Durán! Fuck you!" Tyson would say. And we'd fall down, laughing our asses off.

We stayed up there for several months, bouncing between Los Angeles and Paso Robles, while Tyson used to go back to Phoenix, where he lived. My son was training for a fight nearby, so I told him to come up and stay with me.

Eventually, we had to get on with the business of the fight and headed back to Vero Beach, where McGirt was training his guys. And still Tyson wanted me to train him.

I go to the gym. He's on his cell phone. I say, "Let's hit

the heavy bag." He doesn't want to. Does he want to spar? No. "What do you want to do?"

"Hit the speed bag."

"Okay," I say, "but tomorrow we are going to change the schedule."

The next day, one of his handlers brings him his cell phone: "It's your wife. You've got a new baby."

"New father!" Tyson's shouting. "New father!" He says he doesn't want to train that day.

At five the next morning my alarm rings. Time to get Tyson to go run on the beach. When I knock, the door opens by itself. "Tyson, it's me, Durán. You ready?" Big apartment. No one there.

The day after that, Tyson calls me at two a.m. "Durán, I'm with my wife. I'm not going to train for a while."

"Where are you?"

"Phoenix."

Tyson eventually showed up again in Miami, saying he'd hurt his leg, but one day at the gym he threw his cane away. I still have it somewhere.

Tyson ended up losing to McBride. He quit on his stool after the sixth round. His corner had begged the referee to stop the fight. Afterward, Tyson said he was retiring: "I don't have the guts to fight anymore. My heart is not in it. I don't want to disrespect the sport I love." He wanted to be a good father, he said, and wanted to take care of his children. It was the right decision. He'd lost three of his last four fights by knockout.

That was not the Tyson everyone knew, everyone feared—but it happens. Age catches up with you. I knew that in my own heart, but our hearts also tell us we're boxers, champions, warriors, and we keep chasing that last fight, just one final moment of glory in the ring.

TWELVE

THE

LAST

GOOD-BYES

In the summer of 2006, I got a call from my friend Pupi. "Hey, Durán—you need to come to Miami. The old man is very sick. He could die at any time." He was talking about my old friend Victor del Corral, who'd been by my side since the very beginning of my journey.

I went right away. Victor was at Jackson Memorial Hospital, and his daughter Sonia was with him. It was clear he couldn't recognize anyone and didn't know what was going on. "Look, Papi," said Sonia, "it's Durán." It was the last time I saw him.

The next day, Sonia called and said Victor had died. He was eighty-four. I went to the funeral home where his body had been laid out; around the casket were mementoes and photos of Victor with all his friends, including me. It was a typical Cuban wake and lasted all night, with lots of people talking, drinking coffee, and paying their respects to the man who'd looked after us so well in his restaurant all those years.

After the funeral, I went to the Manhattan restaurant one more time to say good-bye in my own way. It felt wrong to be there without Victor being around, and I didn't want his family to think I was taking advantage of our friendship by continuing to eat for free. How lucky I'd been to know this special man. He was the best—the very best. May he rest in peace.

Victor wasn't the only one to leave us. Toti, Plomo, Arcel, Freddie Brown, Flaco Bala—they've all gone, a sign that time is passing more quickly nowadays. Once upon a time, we thought we were all going to be together forever. Not anymore.

These days, death is never far away from me. In May 2009, I was at home in Panama when the telephone rang at midnight.

"It's me, Tyson."

"The boxer?"

"*Sí*. The boxer." I hadn't heard from him for years—not since we'd been training together. He was in tears, going crazy.

His four-year-old daughter Exodus had just died—it was a terrible story. Her brother Miguel had found her dangling from an exercise treadmill, tangled in a power cable, unconscious. She'd died the next day when she was taken off life support.

"Durán, please, get me Flex," said Tyson. Flex was a Panamanian reggaeton artist. "My daughter was a big fan of his, and I want him to come sing at the service. Whatever he asks, I'll pay."

De Cubas was able to track Flex down and Robin brought him to see me. Flex said he was already committed that day.

"You know how many people would love to sing at the service for Tyson's daughter?" I told him. "God put you in this moment. There were a lot of great singers He could have picked, but He chose you. You're the man."

At the private service, attended only by family and special guests, Flex sang an acoustic version of "Dime Si Te Vas con Él" (Tell Me If You Go with Him) with the choir, and from what I was told, everyone in the congregation was crying, even those who didn't understand Spanish.

"Exodus had a funeral worthy of a dignitary," Tyson would write later. "I didn't realize it until then, but I suddenly knew the deep reason that I had always loved Durán. There is no way I could ever repay him."

Flex didn't charge Tyson a dime.

I was now living comfortably in retirement, still in the same house Eleta bought for me in 1972 after I beat Buchanan. I'd returned to El Cangrejo a hero still. In a strange twist of events, Martín Torrijos, the kid I knew from El Chorrillo, was now president of Panama! It was he who commissioned the statue in my honor that now stands a few blocks from my house, with a plaque that reads *En Honor a Roberto Durán S. "Mano de Piedra." Seis Veces Campeón del Mundo. La Leyenda.* In Honor of Roberto Durán. "Mano de

Piedra." Six-Time World Champion. The Legend. I'm not going to argue with that.

Look at the legacy. There were the Four Kings: Durán, Leonard, Hagler, and Hearns. Between 1980 and 1989, we gave boxing fans everything and more when we fought each other nine times altogether, all spectacular fights. We were all stars, and we all wanted to beat the shit out of each other. We shook hands and then we fought. We hated each other's guts and now we smile, pose for pictures, and have a drink together every so often. That's boxing.

Maybe it's better to say it *was* boxing, because we'll never see another era like it. Fans had a ringside seat to history. It was, as the Americans say, the Golden Age of Boxing, and me, Hearns, Leonard, and Hagler were at the center of it, trading blows, drawing blood. If we'd fought in different times, each of us could have ruled the sport all by ourselves. Instead, we beat each other up, snatching title belts when we could. That's why we're remembered so fondly.

Hagler had left the sport first, in 1987, pissed off at losing to Leonard. He'd fought sixty-seven times, with three losses and two draws. Leonard had retired in 1997 with a 36–3–1 record. Hearns would fight all the way into 2006, retiring with a 61–5–1 record. But I outlasted them all. I won 103 fights.

In 2014, there was a promotional tour for the Kimball book *Four Kings*, and Leonard told me Marvin Hagler didn't want to come and he didn't know why. Hagler was still upset, I told him, because he'd beaten him back in 1987. "Damn right I did," said Leonard.

It also turned out that for years and years Leonard had had a complex about our fight in New Orleans. It made him really angry, I think, that nobody gave him credit for beating me. He knew he didn't beat me when I was doing all right: he beat me because it was not my night and I turned away in a split-second decision I never knew would haunt me for so long or have such consequences for both of us. Instead of making him look good, it had made him look bad. He'd had it on his conscience ever since and had been searching for some way of living with it.

So, thirty-three years after the fight, a filmmaker came to make a documentary about "*No más*," and we met once again. It was going to be the film's big ending, and as we faced each other in a ring in Panama, I could see how uncomfortable he was, the frustration in his eyes when he looked at me, but he didn't hate me anymore. A lot of water has passed under the bridge, and at least now we've come to terms with the past. We see each other quite a bit—on promotional tours, events in Vegas, stuff like that—as friends. I used to call him my black brother. We can look at each other now with respect and love.

But out of all the Four Kings, I'd put my legacy the highest. Never mind the great victories, look at all the accolades. I received *The Ring* magazine's Comeback of the Year award for 1983 and 1989—the only fighter to win it twice. In 1999, the Associated Press ranked me as the greatest lightweight and the seventh-greatest fighter of the twentieth century. In 2001, *The Ring* ranked me as the greatest lightweight of all time. In 2002, it had me as the fifth-best fighter of the past eighty years. El Diablo, Manos de Piedra. A Latin badass. That's why they put me in the International Boxing Hall of Fame in New York.

It's why they put me in the Nevada Boxing Hall of Fame, too, where I was inducted in 2014 by none other than Sugar Ray Leonard. Because my English is very limited, my daughter Irichelle stood up and spoke for me. "Ever since I can remember, our life has been about boxing. Growing up a Durán kid was not always easy, because it involved a lot of sacrifice. And at an age when you need your parents, a lot of times he wasn't there. But we always supported him because we knew he was working for our future."

"I would like to thank America," I then told the audience. "America gave me so much. America put up with me for five decades. I'm very thankful for that." I was so grateful for that moment, and to be able to share it with Irichelle and Robin.

Leonard and I shared a big hug. "Congratulations, my champion," he said. "Congratulations, my friend."

In 2011, I opened a restaurant a few blocks from where I live called La Tasca de Durán, serving traditional Panamanian dishes. It's done pretty well—of course, we get a lot of people coming because of my name.

We've decorated the place with all sorts of memorabilia: my old gloves, championship belts, boxing trunks, boots— even an imprint of my hands, *manos de piedra!* It's like a museum inside a restaurant. I have tapes of all my famous fights running on a continuous loop: the first fight against Leonard, the victory over Barkley, the victory over Buchanan. The walls are covered with great pictures documenting my career: me with Sugar Ray Leonard, me with Manny Pacquiao, me with Mike Tyson, with Floyd Mayweather, Jr. With Sylvester Stallone during the filming of *Rocky II*. Me with movie stars, and with all the great champions.

There may be a whole lot of pictures at my restaurant, but there is only one scale. It stands out on the patio in front of the restaurant and it's one of my proudest possessions. This scale has a lot of history. Many great champions like Ismael Laguna and Ñato Marcel have stepped onto it. But it's precious to me because I weighed in for all of my professional fights on it, from when I started until when I finished. A few years ago the people at the WBC were going to throw it away, but a friend of mine rescued it for me. It would look a lot better if it hadn't been painted, just left it as it was back then, but there you are.

In October 2012, Don King showed up at the restaurant. I had no warning—I'd already gone home for the night and was almost asleep when they called to tell me.

"*Mi hijo!*"—My son!—King exclaimed when I got there. I gave him a hug. "*Mi boxeador! Manos de Piedra! Manos de Piedra!*" After dinner, he went into the kitchen and gave each of the staff $100. The busboys got $100, too, and so did the valet guy.

We should all go see Eleta, King said, he wasn't well. I

had mixed feelings, but finally I said, "What the hell—let's go make peace with him." He was an old man who wasn't going to live much longer. Why bear grudges?

The next day, we found Eleta propped up in a chair with an oxygen mask on. We posed for pictures, had a lot of laughs, but it was also bittersweet, even kind of weird, with Don King sitting on one couch and Eleta and me on another. I was happy to see them, but something felt strange. It's still hard to explain. It wasn't a grudge but maybe resentment. These guys had been with me through the good times, but when the bad times came, they hadn't stuck around. It didn't help that as we were leaving, Eleta grabbed Robin by the arm and said, "You look so much like your father when he was young. It's unbelievable—I got flashbacks from thirty years ago by looking at you." I left knowing I didn't need to see Eleta again—there really was nothing left to say. By January of the next year, he was gone, at ninety-five.

I don't worry about death myself; there are plenty of people to do the worrying for me. But when I went to the doctor and discovered I had a hernia, I was forced to confront the weight issue. It happens to all boxers when they retire, especially those like me who've struggled with their weight throughout their career. I was now over 260 pounds, the heaviest I'd ever been, and, the doctor told me, a prime candidate for a heart attack. So I decided it would be a good idea to have gastric bypass surgery to solve the problem once and for all, and I had some great friends and fans who would pick up the bill.

It was tough to go through, and took a long time to recover from, but in the end I got my weight down to 170 pounds, which I've managed to keep to for a few years now. If only I'd known that a gastric band would help me make weight, I'd have had one inserted while I was fighting! Now Fula takes me every year to the Punta Pacífica medical center for a full examination: head, heart—everything. "Roberto, you can still fight!" the doctor always says. "You have the heart of a twenty-five-year-old! And your brain's fine." That makes me very happy, as, these days, some people say that Hands of Stone is gone in the head because of boxing, which is bullshit. Maybe I was born cracked, but it's not because I've been hit once too often.

These days, life is good in Panama, and that's enough for me. I love it here. People are always asking me why I don't do more, but I say to them: Why make your life complicated? We've lived in the same house for forty-one years now, and I couldn't imagine living anywhere else. We began to fix it up after the first Sugar Ray Leonard fight, and now it's a three-story home with seven bedrooms, a studio, a bar, and a pool. I still have the heavy bags, along with the weight machines. Out front, I have my cars and, behind them, six big Roman statues I bought a long time ago because they reminded me of Caesars Palace in Las Vegas.

Chavo lives in it, too, with his wife, as does one of my younger sons, Brambi. My family is still very close, and they take good care of me. Happily, my mother is still alive, at the age of ninety, and playing the lottery just like she did when

I was growing up. She lives a long way away in San Miguelito, which is a bitch to get to, so I don't see her very often, and when I do, she asks for money! Some things never change! On weekends I usually hook up with friends like Wiwa, who's been loyal to me all these years, ever since he was one of my *manzanillos*. My best friend is still Chaparro, but he lives a long way away, too, and I don't see him so much.

Most of my kids are grown now, and very independent. Irichelle and Jovanna live in Miami, and I'm fortunate that Robin's here in Panama looking out for me—in 2010, I bought a BMW 7 Series and asked the dealership to fit neon lights underneath it and paint my face on the hood. "Dad, it's a BMW," said Robin. "It's not a hot rod." I still wish I could find a body shop to paint my face on it.

I have three other children with three other women. These things happen: I'm just a man. Once you get exposed to the level of fame I've reached, you're going to have women jumping on you whether you're married or not—crazy shit. But at the end of the day, a celebrity is just a human being. Fortunately, my wife forgave me. When you love someone, you forgive everything. Sharing the good and the bad, that's the key to any marriage.

One of these three kids, Dalia Durán, is actually my first child. I still see her when I go to Miami. I met the mother of the second child in a nightclub in Miami; she said she was on the pill, but she got pregnant, and my son Alcibíades Durán was born. I don't see him or his mother now—the last I heard, he was in the army. Then there was a woman in Chitré, in Panama—she also said she was on the pill, but she gave birth to my daughter Viviana Durán. She's about twelve now, but I don't see her much. All I do is send her mother child support payments.

Viviana's the only child who is afraid of me. One day, she'll find out who her father is and come looking for me so we can talk. If she wants to call me papa, okay; but if she doesn't, I don't need it—that's life. Remember how I grew up. The idea of having a complex about your father? Nah—I'm not into that.

Some people may look down on the way my life's turned out, but everyone in Panama knows my family situation, and I don't care what people think.

Most days, I hang out at my restaurant. I recommend the food there. We have three very good soups—a hammy chickpea-and-cabbage combination, a black bean soup, and a garlic soup with a poached egg floating in the middle. One of my favorite dishes is *sancocho de gallina*, which is made with chicken, yuca, and *mazorca* (corn on the cob). Fula cooks it for me every day. Then there's the *tamal cubano*—seasoned cornmeal flecked with red peppers, steamed in a corn husk. Or you can have eggs with rice, *arroz con carne*, or *frijoles*— they're more of my favorites.

I'll grab a beer or a whiskey and sit down and watch the tapes of my fights with customers—I love to see myself kicking Leonard's ass again, or Barkley's, or Davey Moore's, and listen to people talk as though it happened yesterday. I pose for pictures with ugly old guys, young pretty girls, babies, and celebrities who've visited, like the singer Usher. There's even a picture of me at a promotional event in London posing with a woman who's holding my balls. Her friend had told her I had large balls, so she made a bet with him that I'd let her feel them. I thought she was joking, but she went and grabbed them and said, "You do have the biggest balls!"— and won her bet!

And of course I play with the salsa band. Pototo gets some of the boys together on the weekend and people come from all over to dance salsa with us. I always get up and sing a few songs—what gringos would call a "salsa riff," with improvised lyrics.

Plata, money, is just as much of an issue for me as it's always been. I'm happy when I've got some, just as happy without it—that's my problem, which means I'm always looking out for it. I prefer cash, not checks or contracts where you get paid only now and then: money up front—that's how it should be. I used to love it when Don King gave me those $1,000 bonuses! When I run out of money, I sometimes borrow from my friends, because I know Fula wouldn't give me any. But I always pay them back the next day.

These days, I can make money going to the United States and the UK to sign autographs. In London especially, people are big fans and very generous. The first time I went I thought they'd be pissed off with me for beating their idol

Ken Buchanan, but they adore me—I've seen guys with tattoos of my face! It's too bad I never fought in the UK—I'd love to have fought for them.

Every time I visit the UK, the support is amazing. In 2014, I did an event at the Grosvenor Casino in Newcastle and people went crazy. Irichelle came with me to translate, and I loved posing for pictures with all the fans. Of course afterward we went to the bar, and I invited everyone to have a pint with me. They treat me like a star over there, and I like it that I can hang out with them, too, play pool and drink beer.

I've also become friends with one of England's greats, Ricky Hatton. He's a good boxer, but he could have gone further. When he lost to Vyacheslav Senchenko in 2012, I was at the fight. I'd told him to watch down below, and sure enough, the guy knocked him out with a body shot to the kidneys. Exactly what I'd told him—he throws a lot of lefts. But Ricky didn't listen to me: he went in like crazy and the guy took him out with a left hook.

When it comes to business deals, I let my sons or daughter do the work, since I wouldn't know what I was signing and would end up getting screwed. One guy got me to sign over the rights to my life story for all time. Everything—movie, books, the lot. He also wanted to open a boxing gym in Panama and share the profits with me, and was supposed to pay me $7,500 a month plus whatever they made in endorsements. But when Robin eventually read the contract, he explained that the payments of $7,500 were advances against revenue and that the guy would take a 50 percent cut of any endorsement money, and since he hadn't done any business yet and was already a year and a half into the deal, he claimed I owed him $300,000! We had to get an attorney to sort it all out.

Things are no different today. People I haven't heard from in years will suddenly show up in connection with something I signed long ago without knowing what I was doing. Robin says I'm not an easy guy to steer, that I think the street smarts I got when I was young make me a sharp businessman. But they aren't necessarily much use when you've got a whole lot of numbers in front of you and a contract to sign.

In 2012, Robin thought that people outside Panama needed to be reminded of who I was, and had the idea of our family doing a TV reality show. The first series was a great success: people enjoyed following me around and seeing the kind of life I lead now. The best episode was the one in which Robin surprised me with the car I'd loved most of all, the one I'd had to sell back in 1986—an Excalibur. He'd gone looking all over Panama for the very same model, even found the original car I'd had, but the guy wanted $200,000 for it. Robin went to dealerships in disguise so they wouldn't try to rip him off, and finally found one for a good price. While I was hanging out with friends and family outside the restaurant, my son Brambi put his hands over my eyes. After a moment, I heard everyone shout, *"Abre los ojos!"* Open your eyes!

And there it was. Robin pulled up in the car, with a big red bow on the hood. *Chuleta!* My sons hugged and kissed me. I got behind the wheel and we all took off.

The producers wanted to do a second series, but there were some personal issues. Robin had separated from the mother of his two children—sometimes they'd fought on camera in front of everyone in Panama. The gossip column "Chollywood" was trying to dig up some dirt, and the whole business took its toll on us as a family. The program had such great ratings that people knew more about us than we did ourselves, even felt we belonged to them. So we decided to leave it as one successful series. But people still ask for it. We'll see.

In 2013, Robin reached an agreement in the United States for a movie about my life titled *Hands of Stone*, which is coming out in 2016. My old friend Robert De Niro, who I beat at softball in New York all those years ago, is playing Ray Arcel, while Usher is Sugar Ray Leonard and my friend Rubén Blades is Eleta. And the most important role, of course, *me*, belongs to Édgar Ramírez, a Venezuelan actor. We had all the cast for dinner and drinks at the restaurant, and they got a good taste of the kinds of salsa parties we often throw on weekends.

And in the fall of 2015, Robin was chosen to play me in *Manos de Piedra: Un K.O. Musical,* telling my life story through the eyes of people on the streets of El Chorrillo. It had a budget of more than $400,000, a cast of thirty-eight, and they re-created some of the big fights like Leonard and

Barkley. Robin did a great job. I went to see it when it opened in Panama and got up onstage to thank the audience. The critics hailed it as a major success, and Fula isn't the only one to cry every time she's seen it.

People think I'm a millionaire but I'm not, although I used to be. I think I made about $60 million from my fights, but nowadays the house is all that's left to show for it. The cash I do have goes to paying the bills, for food, water, and electricity, with a little bit put aside in case of an emergency. The days of buying fancy cars and microlights are long gone! But still people come knocking on my door for money even though they know that it's been years since I had a payout from a fight and, Panama being the place it is, that I've had money problems.

Some people feel sorry for me; they think that growing up on the streets has been a burden I've carried all my life. But I don't know any different—I have nothing to compare it to. It hasn't been an easy life, but it's the life I've had. The only one. I'm not sitting around with a psychiatrist, trying to figure out why my dad abandoned me. I'm not traumatized by anything I went through. If you like me, fine. If not, let's move on—it's all the same to me. People ask me what I'd do differently the second time around and I tell them, "Nothing." I don't do regrets. Why? Because nobody is born knowing what's going to happen. Only God knows that.

But I'm happy. Some of the stories I've been telling you about my life might have made you cry, but you'll have found yourself laughing, too. No tears for me, though: I'm not finished yet. I'm going to die of old age, it's quite clear to me. That's written by God. I've survived a car crash, an airplane crash, a motorcycle crash, and I'm still going. When I die, the doctors will have to open me up to see what I'm made of. I should have been dead a long time ago, but God doesn't want me dead. El Cholo will live forever.

ACKNOWLEDGMENTS

First of all, I would like to thank Mr. George Diaz for taking the time to listen to me, and for understanding my life and all that goes with it. I'm not an easy person, because I'm always in a rush, but he was patient and somehow made it work. George also took the time to do his homework and research my real life—not just the bullshit written in some books or the misinformation that's on the Web. He went beyond all that and connected with my son Robin and my wife, Felicidad.

You know by now that I've had a tough life, but also a beautiful one. I've lived how I've wanted to live and done most of the things I've wanted to do, and yet I've still been a family man. I've had a lot of money, only to lose it and get it back. I've been lied to, scammed, and robbed by people I've trusted, but I've also had the love of my family, who have been with me through thick and thin. My wife—oh, my wife—she should be getting the belts and statues. She's the one person I really depend on.

My heart resides in my country, Panama. It's where I was born and raised, and it's where I will die. Even if, at times, I've felt betrayed by my country or unloved by those I've fought for, I harbor no hate or grudges. On the contrary, I love my country, and every time I went into battle, all I was thinking of was triumphing for my people. At the end of the day, I'm just a man. I've made bad decisions like any other person, but I don't regret any of them, because without them I wouldn't be the man I've become, and I probably wouldn't have fought with such hunger for those championships. I'm still that young boy from the streets whose childhood was taken by his rough life, and I'm still that young man who won his first world title in New York City. I will never change that. Thank you, George, for telling the world my story in my own words. This is the life of Roberto "Manos de Piedra" Durán. This is the life of a son of Panama.

—Roberto Duran

In 1971, a few days after my fifteenth birthday, I stepped into the old Miami Jai-Alai Fronton with my uncle to watch the first Ali–Frazier fight on a giant screen. I became mesmerized that day by the blood sport of boxing, a form of warfare equal parts physical and psychological.

I eventually made my way to ringside as a journalist for some of the most dramatic moments in boxing history, including the infamous "Bite Fight" in Las Vegas. On that summer night in 1997, Mike Tyson found a crazy way out against Evander Holyfield.

The ultimate bad-ass, in a fit of frustration, looked for an exit strategy.

Wasn't that also the narrative of Roberto Durán in one of the most iconic fights in boxing history? It is easy to paint with broad strokes when defining our sports heroes, although we like to color within the lines. Good or bad? Winner or loser? Strong or weak?

Roberto Durán was all those things during his career. I've tried to be true to his story, and he certainly pulled no punches in trying to explain his complicated and conflicted journey in boxing and as a hero to the people of Panama.

It was a complicated journey for me, too, trying to piece things together with Roberto. Like any good boxer, he has learned to move on, and not get stuck in the past. Always look to the next round. But we found a way, thanks in large measure to his wonderful family—including his wife, Fula, son Robin, and daughter Irichelle. They helped Roberto and me put the pieces together, and the whole family had the conviction to reveal hard truths that were not always flattering. Thank you, Roberto, for being true to yourself after all these years—a mix of kindness, quirkiness, obstinacy, tenacity, and humor.

Thank you, too, Sugar Ray Leonard, for your role in telling the story, and helping to weave a narrative for a man who was once your greatest enemy, and whom you now call one of your best friends.

And many thanks to my better half, Theresa—always my best friend, always my most supportive fan on this and every other project I've undertaken.

A book, much like life, is a collaborative journey. People come into the plot. Some leave. Some stay. Regardless, they shape your story. Through circumstances and serendipity, Roberto Durán came into my life. Together, we told his story. I hope you enjoyed reading it.

—George Diaz

CREDITS FOR PHOTO INSERT

Page 1, top: *The Ring* Magazine/Getty Images; bottom left and right: Bettmann/Getty Images

Page 2, top: *The Ring* Magazine/Getty Images; bottom: Bettmann/Getty Images

Page 3, top and bottom: Bettmann/Getty Images

Page 4, top and bottom: *The Ring* Magazine/Getty Images

Page 5, top: Private Collection/Photo © Christie's Images/Bridgeman Images; bottom: *The Ring* Magazine/Getty Images

Page 6, top left: *The Ring* Magazine/Getty Images; top right and bottom: Ron Galella, Ltd./WireImage

Page 7, top: *The Ring* Magazine/Getty Images; bottom: John Iacono/*Sports Illustrated*/Getty Images

Page 8, top left: Focus on Sport/Getty Images; top right: Manny Millan/*Sports Illustrated*/Getty Images; bottom: Bettmann/Getty Images

Page 9, top: Bettmann/Getty Images; bottom: *The Ring* Magazine/Getty Images

Page 10, top: New York *Daily News* Archive via Getty Images; bottom: *The Ring* Magazine/Getty Images

Page 11, top and bottom: Bettmann/Getty Images

Page 12, top: Trinity Mirror/Mirrorpix/Alamy Stock Photo; bottom: Donaldson Collection/Michael Ochs Archives/Getty Images

Page 13, top and bottom: Bettmann/Getty Images

Page 14, top: Cindy Karp/The *Life* Images Collection/Getty Images; bottom: Steve Starr/CORBIS/Corbis via Getty Images

Page 15, top: Ron Galella, Ltd./WireImage; bottom: *The Ring* Magazine/Getty Images

Page 16, top: Anna Zieminski/AFP/Getty Images; bottom: Ethan Miller/Getty Images